KEEPING
HOUSE

KEEPING HOUSE

A 30-Day Meditation on the
Value of Housekeeping

Christy Fitzwater

© 2022 by Christy Fitzwater

Published by christyfitzwater.com

Cover design by Josiah Gardner

All rights reserved. No part of this publication may be reproduced, stored in a retrieval system, or transmitted in any form or by any means—for example, electronic, photocopy, recording—without the prior written permission of the publisher. The only exception is brief quotations in printed reviews.

ISBN 9798766398998 (paperback)

All Scripture quotations are taken from the Holy Bible, New International Version®, NIV®. Copyright ©1973, 1978, 1984, 2011 by Biblica, Inc.™ Used by permission of Zondervan. All rights reserved worldwide. www.zondervan.com The "NIV" and "New International Version" are trademarks registered in the United States Patent and Trademark Office by Biblica, Inc.™

"Don't you feel that it is pleasanter to help one another, to have daily duties which make leisure sweet when it comes, and to bear and forebear, that home may be comfortable and lovely to us all?"

~ Louisa May Alcott, *Little Women*

CONTENTS

Introduction 9
1. Get Therapy 13
2. Discover the Treasure of Solitude 17
3. Benefit from Humility 23
4. Strengthen Your Body 29
5. Allow for Perfection 33
6. Tend to the Linens 39
7. Bring the Light 45
8. Delight Them 49
9. Preach the Gospel 53
10. Expect Your Family to Help 57
11. Be Honest 61
12. Anticipate Needs 67
13. Include the Beautiful 73
14. Create Good Smells 79
15. Give Yourself a Gift 85

16. Make Repairs 89
17. Be Efficient..95
18. Simplify 101
19. Waste Not 107
20. Manage the Fridge...113
21. Practice Hospitality 117
22. Clean Smarter 123
23. Send a Message...129
24. Stay in Motion 135
25. Bestow Honor 141
26. Grow Something 147
27. Raise the Valuation.......................................153
28. Know When to Neglect.................................159
29. Rub in Gratitude...165
30. Keep Improving Your Craft 171
Endnotes..177

INTRODUCTION

I did not expect, at the age of 52, to be unemployed and looking for work. I certainly never expected the job opportunity that came my way. One Sunday, my husband Matt asked a friend why his wife wasn't in church with him, and the friend replied that his wife was at home, exhausted from cleaning vacation rentals without enough help for most of the summer. She managed several properties, but having lost a full-time employee, she had to do much of the work herself. Hearing this news, I picked up my phone and texted her, asking if she could use a hand.

"Are you kidding me?" she responded. Within minutes, I had myself a temp job, and she had scheduled me to join her for training the next morning.

I thought I would despise this cleaning job. I

thought I was only taking it to help a friend and earn a little money. But it turned out that I actually enjoyed the entire experience and was very sad when it ended after six weeks. As I focused on detailed cleaning in a different setting than my own home, I learned new ways to clean and had a lot of time to think about why this job mattered so much. That temporary employment is what prompted this little book.

Being in so many vacation rentals, either cleaning or staying in them myself over the last few years, has given me an ability to compare and contrast the experience in different homes. One afternoon, my husband and kids were hanging out, and we were talking about different places we've rented.

"Remember the downtown Austin rental?" Caleb said.

"Eeew," we all groaned. That was a windowless, uncomfortable place to sleep and not much more. We got out of there as quickly as we could.

Borrowing someone else's residence for a few days or a week can be life-giving, or it can make you feel like you're just helping someone pay his mortgage. It can make you feel refreshed and cared for, or uncomfortable and anxious to leave. Now that I've been on both sides, as guest and maid, I see how my careful attention as a maid can make or break the guest's experience in the home.

But it's not just the guest's experience that defines the value of routine chores in the house. There is also value for the woman who is stretching to dust the light fixtures above the bathroom sink. She gets something for her mind, body, and soul, too. Before locking the door and leaving, guest and maid alike can look back into the house one more time to say, "This is good."

I want you to know why: Why keep house? What is the value of the housekeeper's role? Where is the joy in doing grimy, unending tasks? Do the details really matter? Come with me for a tour of vacation rentals, and let me share with you some important cleaning ideas and Bible-centered encouragement regarding housekeeping. Whether you're new to this role or you've been doing it for decades, as I have, we can all use a little refresher on method and meaning.

. 1 .

GET THERAPY

It has been a year in which many of my journal entries have had the word *PAIN* scrawled across the top of the page, in all caps. The COVID-19 pandemic was the base layer, and then the Lord allowed layers of suffering to build on top of that: intense work stress, a crippling church crisis, and family illnesses. I ended up resigning from the job I had labored over for seven years.

Hard, hard days. One shocking hit to the gut after another.

Matt and I always pray together before we go to sleep at night. Or rather, whoever is the least stressed prays. But regularly, during such a hard year, we would look at each other, give a weak laugh, and ask, "Who is going to pray tonight? Obviously neither one of us."

Sometimes we would joke about texting his mom and seeing if she would come in and pray over us. We probably should have done that for real.

So, I found myself with this job cleaning vacation rentals. It was supposed to be temp work, to help pay the bills, but it turned out to be unexpected therapy for my weary soul. At the moment in which I am writing this, I am sitting in a cozy rental cabin in the woods, tucked right up against a majestic ridge of the Rocky Mountains. While I'm waiting for the sheets to get through the spin cycle, I can see the pine trees through the window and hear a creek running just below the front deck. The Lord knew just what I needed.

In her book *Suffering Is Never for Nothing*, Elisabeth Elliot describes losing not one but two husbands. Her advice, when one is hit with an unexpected and crushing season of suffering, is to do a simple chore. She encourages her reader not to think about the long road ahead but rather to do some normal household task that is calling for attention in the moment.[2] When my dad died years ago, it was good to do something normal and useful. Going down to the laundry room and sorting socks did provide some restoration for my broken heart.

Here I am today in this beautiful setting, given the opportunity to do the next thing that needs to be done in this vacation rental. I tackle the cleaning chores one at a time: first start laundry and run the dishwasher, then scrub the bathroom, tidy the kitchen, clean out the fridge, dust the rooms one by one, make up the beds, and finally mop the floors. As Elisabeth suggests, I do whatever needs to be done next.

One chore at a time, I busy my hands with useful work that will benefit someone else. I pray as I move about the cabin and let the quiet and the housekeeping do some kind of mysterious healing inside of me. The world might be falling apart out there, but for now I'm folding guest towels: a salve. Crises and pain paralyze our minds and bodies. When we wake up in the morning, grief makes it feel like a really good idea to spend the day under the warmth and safety of the covers. Household chores help us move—literally—just like a physical therapist comes in just hours after someone's orthopedic surgery and says, "Okay, let's get you up and walking." It's hard to maneuver while in pain, but it's that movement that brings a speedy recovery. And recovery is what we crave.

There have been times during this year of tremendous difficulty that I would say to myself, "Woman, get up out of this bed and start a load of laundry." With herculean effort, I would swing my legs off the edge of the bed and move toward the hamper. I would only think about starting that one task, not any further ahead in the future than that. I began to create a tiny bit of momentum, and that momentum would help me move from the laundry room to the kitchen, doing the next chore that needed to be done. Chores were a way to move forward, both physically and emotionally.

If you have had a year to beat all years, housekeeping is inexpensive therapy. Do one task. When you've done that, you'll probably feel a little bit better and maybe ready to do one more task. Move yourself into a healthier emotional state by doing simple housework.

. 2 .

DISCOVER THE TREASURE OF SOLITUDE

Teaching high school Spanish taxed my introverted brain to its limits. A forty-three-minute class could mean dozens of different interactions with students, from responding to "May I go to the bathroom?" to throwing the quintessential teacher's evil eye toward the guys messing around at the back table. Interspersed throughout all those interactions, I managed to teach Spanish lessons.

Last year, due to an increase in students, I was forced to give up having my own classroom and to teach instead from a traveling cart. This meant that my prep time and lunch hour were spent parked in a busy hall right next to the student bathrooms. It was a year of no quiet and no breaks from interacting. You can understand, then, how precious it was when I got that cleaning job the following summer and spent hours by myself.

A couple days a week, I was working three hours alone, in a cabin in the woods or a condo on a mountain, and on either side of that work was a half-hour drive to get to those more remote locations. What would I do with all this travel and cleaning time? At first, I packed my AirPods, thinking I would fill the time with listening to podcasts or music. I did some of that, but mostly I ended up turning them off and letting my brain roam free, while putting my back into my work.

Last Christmas, I read *Mastermind: How to Think Like Sherlock Holmes* by Maria Konnikova. She described Holmes's habit of stopping when problems were most in a knot, and doing something completely unrelated, such as playing a musical instrument or smoking a pipe—some activity that required thought but not too much thought. This enabled his mind to work problems while he was distracted. Maria says that our brains keep working while we're doing these kinds of activities.[3] What better activity for the brain than doing house chores? For me, this means scrubbing at splatters on the mirror with a Norwex cloth (put one on your shopping list) and not listening to anything on my phone. It's quiet in the bathroom, and my concentration on cleaning the mirror is just what my tired brain needs to continue thinking through what troubles me most.

But there's more to it than that. My brain is not alone. As a follower of Christ, his Spirit dwells in me. My problems are his problems. I pray off and on while I work, and I believe that when I focus in on housekeeping and running the vacuum over the floor, the Spirit is working in my subconscious. (Doesn't Psalm 139 tell us there's absolutely nowhere that God can't follow us?) All the scriptures I have memorized are tucked away in what Sherlock describes as "the brain attic."[3] God's Spirit pulls out those memory verses, dusts them off, and his truth permeates the problem I'm working in my mind, whether consciously or subconsciously.

The story of Mary and Martha always shows up in conversations about housework. Think about the fact that, in order to spend time with Jesus, Mary physically had to stop working and go sit at Jesus' feet. He applauded her decision. But now we have his Spirit inside us. We can clean the house in a flurry, in preparation for company, while enjoying the presence of Jesus and his words inside our minds. We can choose "what is better" (Luke 10:42) by listening to him and talking to him and asking him questions while unloading the dishwasher, folding a load of towels, or sweeping off the front porch. The solitude of housework becomes a mental opportunity to sit at the feet of Jesus, if we will purposefully look to him with our minds.

I'm cleaning vacation rentals, which means I'm cleaning an entire house in a few hours. Then, a few days later, I have to come back and clean it all again—change all the sheets again, wash all the towels, mop all the floors. Housekeeping is the definition of monotony. But the solitude found in those hours of repetition is a greater treasure than many people might ever experience in more "meaningful" jobs. As we pull out the cleaning bucket, we should ask, "What is my brain going to do while I'm cleaning?" And we can put away the phone and the AirPods, at least for a good chunk of time, and let our minds do the wonderful work God created them to do.

Do you know what happened during my weeks of solitude while cleaning vacation rentals? God inspired my mind to write this book. I always carry a little notebook in my purse, and one day I wrote down chapter ideas every time I passed by it. I would clean the shower and think of an idea, wipe out the sink and think of an idea, toss another load into the dryer and think of an idea. This book was born in hours and hours of silence. I wonder—I just wonder—what God might work in your mind, if you would refuse to entertain your brain while you clean your house and would designate those hours for purposeful solitude instead. What problems could be solved by worshipping while cleaning? How many people could you pray for? Solitude is a treasure waiting to be found by the woman who keeps house.

. 3 .
BENEFIT FROM HUMILITY

What makes for a noble profession? For years I would say, "I'm a high school teacher," and people would speak words of respect like "I don't know how teachers do such a hard job" or "What great work it is to be a teacher."

Then I resigned from teaching. It was during the second summer of the pandemic, when every single store had "help wanted" ads in the window, many of them with signing bonuses. I was unemployed and needed a little income but didn't want anything relationally stressful. I definitely wanted a job that was confined to the work hours, unlike teaching, which is wonderful but 24/7. I looked around at a multitude of job options, but pride rose up in my heart. How could I go from the admired position of teacher to making sandwiches or checking groceries? That would feel like a humiliating demotion.

But the checkbook kept saying to me, "Hey sister, you need a little income."

One summer day, my mother-in-law and her sister hosted a luncheon for a bunch of women from church, and they invited me to come. I sat next to a woman whom I had recently met. As we ate, she told us some of her story. Her father had been a prisoner of war in Europe. Seeking a better life, he and her mother had moved to the United States and then worked their way out of poverty into the American Dream. She told me she had started working hard in the home at the age of three, because her parents were working opposite schedules, and she was needed to help out around the house.

"I've always worked hard," she told me.

This daughter of immigrants humbled me with her story, and it changed my feelings of pride and the way I was looking at my unemployed status.

A few weeks after this luncheon, my husband came home and told me about my friend's need for cleaning help. The thought of cleaning vacation rentals sounded about as unpleasant and humiliating as work could get, but I thought of the woman who had started working at the age of three and considered how hard her parents had worked to create a good life for their family. If they could work that hard, surely I could do some grunt work—that I would probably hate—for a season, to make our financial life less tight. And nobody had to know that I would be cleaning toilets. I could keep my dignity intact.

My first job was to help clean a two-bedroom, two-bath condominium. By the end of the day, I was tired. But it felt good to work with my hands—surprisingly good. And I was shocked at the rewarding feelings I was experiencing. I didn't hate the work.

In fact, not only did I not hate the work, but I'm sitting here six weeks later asking the Lord if, hmmm, maybe this is good long-term work for me? I've gone from feeling like cleaning rentals was horrible, demeaning work, to considering it to be extremely rewarding work. It's so different from teaching, but it's good and noble in its own way. I've found myself proudly telling friends, "I'm cleaning vacation rentals," and even posting pictures on social media of the beautiful scenery around these mountain cabins I'm getting to clean.

A few weeks into this cleaning gig, Matt and I took a vacation to Wyoming. When we walked into our hotel room, my first thought was to appreciate the housekeeper who had readied the room for us. On the bed were two washcloths, rolled and shaped into a heart.

On top was an envelope and an invitation to leave a tip for the person who had cleaned our room. I immediately went to find cash. Because our housekeeper had done an excellent job, we felt comfortable as guests. The bed was neatly made. The room was tidy. The bathroom was spotless. I was picturing all that I would have had to do, if I had been the cleaner, and I was filled with thankfulness for the person who was willing to humble herself or himself to take a job that created a pleasant vacation experience for us. The work was of new value to me.

Jesus was willing to do grunge work, and he encouraged us to do the same for others.

> So he got up from the meal, took off his outer clothing, and wrapped a towel around his waist. After that, he poured water into a basin and began to wash his disciples' feet, drying them with the towel that was wrapped around him (John 13:4-5).

The dirty work.

"Do you understand what I have done for you?" Jesus asks. "I have set you an example that you should do as I have done for you" (John 13:12b, 15). *Should someone who has a college degree stoop to cleaning a toilet for someone?* I had been quietly asking myself. The true answer is found in Jesus' demonstration of humility. The low work—the undesirable work—is where we begin to understand his heart.

Cleaning hairballs out of shower drains and scrubbing toilets is not glamorous, but there's an end product to cleaning that is of high value. The teachers who invest in children are doing great work, but so are the moms who clean bathrooms and fold clean underwear while their kids are learning. Both jobs create a good life for families, don't they? What more noble work is there than that? Our definitions of valuable work can be rewritten to include the household tasks that appear humiliating and come with no hourly wage, but at the end of the day come together to create a clean, peaceful space for our precious families.

. 4 .

STRENGTHEN YOUR BODY

Matt called at noon, and I burst into tears of exhaustion. It was my first time cleaning the mountain condo, and I had hit a wall. "I'm so tired," I wailed into the phone. You would think I had just climbed Everest or something.

This condo was on a third story, it had a set of stairs to a loft bedroom, and the laundry was on the subfloor. I had been running five flights of stairs all morning, to say nothing of the physical cleaning I was doing between laundry runs. Up until then, my exercise had been lacking over the summer and I was not prepared for that kind of exertion. My feet were blistered from jogging stairs multiple times, and at one point, I hung my arms over a top bunk bed and cried like a baby because I had zero energy left to make that cursed thing.

Matt talked me through my blubbering, and we finally agreed that I should go home and rest, and then the two of us would return in the evening and finish up the last of the cleaning. That was no small offer on his part, because it was a half-hour drive from our house. But I'm pretty sure he would have agreed to anything, if it would stop his wife's dripping tears.

I felt better later when I was texting a twenty-something who was doing the same work, and she told me she had no idea when she took the job how exhausting it would be. Okay, so it wasn't just this fifty-something wimp who was having a hard time with the workload. Carrying laundry, reaching into showers to wipe down walls, stretching to fit sheets on a bed, and pushing a vacuum and a mop are cardio activities.

Years ago, I used to type medical reports for an occupational therapist. When someone was injured, he would have to reenter his job slowly and become what the therapists referred to as "work hardened." People have to get in shape physically in order to perform their jobs at peak energy levels.

When I started cleaning vacation rentals, the work came with a timer. Because I was getting paid by the hour, I had to put my hand to the plow and not stop working. It made me realize how much dilly-dallying I do when I'm cleaning my own home. It hasn't been uncommon practice for me to start cleaning a room and then take a break to check email or read a chapter in a book. But when I walk into a rental cabin, I know that it requires exercise to get this entire place spit-spot and turned around for the next guest in time. It's fast-paced, as I set a steady rhythm between the washer and dryer and cleaning the rooms. It gets my heart rate up, and that is very good for my body.

Someone said, "Now that you're cleaning for a living, do you hate coming home and having to clean?" The answer was no. I've actually learned that moving around and cleaning several rooms in a few hours gets the job done quickly and also benefits my body at the same time. It has motivated me to do the same thing at my own house. I can move quickly through several rooms, going back and forth to the laundry room and working up a sweat.

The other day, I was talking to my mom about how much we need to exercise but we really hate it. We're book-reading, indoorsy women. But I told her I have realized, over the years, that I enjoy exercise when it's accomplishing something. I like to mow the lawn and rake leaves and pull weeds. She commented that there used to be a day when women got their exercise by working hard. They didn't need a gym membership because their everyday lives were their workout. We can return to that, to some extent, if we block out a few hours for cleaning and really get after it. And you know what? There's no gym fee for housekeepers. No contract to sign. You don't have to buy cute leggings or layered tanks. It's free exercise. If we'll just put our backs into it and stay on task the way professional cleaners do, we can make keeping house a regular workout routine.

. 5 .

ALLOW FOR PERFECTION

The door to the cabin was open to let in the fresh summer air, so I could see the owner of the rental cabin walking over from her house. We had never met before, and I was instantly nervous. My hope was that she was coming to say hello and introduce herself, but she had more in mind than that.

"I'm almost done cleaning," I told her.

This owner swooped in and began a detailed inspection of my work. Though she was kind, her eagle eye was terrifying, and I had an urge to stop everything and write apologies to every Spanish student I had ever had, for each mark of my red pen they had endured.

"This cabinet is a mess," she said, pointing to one smudge on the cabinet door.

"I'll take care of it," I said.

She walked into the bathroom and looked over every detail. Picking up the soap dispenser, she told me I should make sure it's full every time. I informed her that I had already taken care of that. Phew.

I followed this woman into the bedroom, holding my breath, and watched as she pulled back a corner of the bedding I had labored to arrange perfectly.

"Good, you've remembered to put an extra blanket on the bed." She ran her hand over the covers, smoothing out a few minuscule wrinkles I had failed to smooth. (And my husband thinks I'm ridiculously picky when we make the bed together at home!)

Next stop was the living area, where she informed me the bowl on the end table really should be on the coffee table. I yes ma'amed her and promised to fix it. Then she stopped at a lampshade, which was two millimeters crooked, and she instructed me to make sure the lamp shades were perfectly level. "That's how I like them," she said.

Finally, she told me I had done a good job (had I?), and she left. I took in my first full breath and let out an exhale. That was intense.

Later I was talking to my boss, and she said, "Oh yes, she comes every time I clean and does a similar inspection. Sorry, I should have warned you. I hope you weren't too discouraged."

Allow for Perfection

To the contrary, it seemed appropriate that the owner would come and make sure everything was spotless for her next guests. This cabin was beautiful, and the owner had put a lot of effort into making it a comfortable, inviting place for guests. She was paying me good money to make sure it was also clean and perfectly arranged and stocked, so it was fitting that she should have the right to perform a detailed examination of my work.

If I had been cleaning that cabin for my own family, I wouldn't have noticed the finger smudge on the cabinet door and certainly wouldn't have worried about refilling the soap dispenser until we were at the last drop of soap. But I wasn't cleaning the cabin for my own family. I was working for someone else, and it was my job to please this rental owner. This experience made me think of Paul's words to the followers of Christ who were slaves. In Colossians 3:22b-24, he commanded them to work "with sincerity of heart and reverence for the Lord," adding, "Whatever you do, work at it with all your heart, as working for the Lord, not for human masters, since you know that you will receive an inheritance from the Lord as a reward. It is the Lord Christ you are serving." We are not keeping house for our families. We are keeping house for the Lord Christ.

Yesterday I spent the day cleaning my own home.

My husband will never in a million years notice if the lampshade on the bathroom counter is crooked or if I've smoothed the wrinkles out of the bed or if I've refilled the soap dispenser. But I was joyfully cleaning, not only for my own family, but for a greater owner of our home. As I scrubbed and mopped and folded laundry, the Lord and I were in sweet fellowship. The cleaning was for Jesus.

And it's not that Jesus was going to sweep in with a white glove and point out every detail that I had missed. No, what was important was that I could feel his presence as I worked, and I loved him and wanted to please him. Who would see that I carefully vacuumed the baseboard? My Lord and Savior. We serve a God who sees the details of our lives. I did my best work for him.

Booker T. Washington made an interesting observation about servitude in his book *Up from Slavery*. Having grown up as a slave, Washington experienced emancipation. After a trip to Europe, he wrote, "The English servant expects, as a rule, to be nothing but a servant, and so he perfects himself in the art to a degree that no class of servants in America has yet reached. In our country the servant expects to become, in a few years, a 'master' himself."[4] Washington's commentary makes me ask myself this question: What class of servant am I when it comes to keeping house? Am I chafing against this humble work and longing for the day when I'll break free from it, or have I settled into the position of housekeeper, striving to perfect the art of home management in order to please my master?

A friend told me that when she was growing up, her mom was insanely picky about the housekeeping. Everything had to be perfect. That kind of perfectionism can make us tired and resentful. But being picky *ourselves* and *by choice* because of a sincere heart to please our Creator feels different. It feels warm and meaningful. So, I say yes, there is a place for perfection in keeping house, when it is an act of worship, when every detail is an act of love brought to the altar of our loving Father, and when we say, "I'm doing this for you, Lord." Hospital corners on bed sheets, dusting above the bathroom vanity where no one will ever see, and vacuuming minuscule crumbs from the couch cushions take on new meaning when it is the Lord Christ we are serving.

. 6 .
TEND TO THE LINENS

The greatest question of all time: Does it really matter if you make the bed every day? If you say no, evidently you did not grow up with my mother. When I was growing up, brushing one's teeth and making one's bed were in the same lofty category of significance.

"If you at least make your bed, the whole room looks better," Mom always says. She makes her bed every day. I would like to point out that Dad went to be with the Lord many years ago, and Mom still makes the bed, even though she often is alone in the house all day and no one sees whether this task is accomplished.

My boss spent a good amount of time giving me a lesson on how to make the beds at a vacation rental. The sheets would always go in the washer first thing, because of course every guest gets clean bedding. We talked about making hospital corners at the foot of the bed, but Mom had taught me to do that when I was young. The top sheet goes on upside down, so you can fold the top edge over the blanket. This creates clean lines at the head of the bed and an invitation to pull down the covers, crawl in, and get a good night of sleep. I was then taught a nifty way to fold the pillow case in on itself, creating a neat, enclosed pillow. At the time, I guffawed and thought to myself, *I would never do that at home*, but I practiced doing it so much when I was cleaning rentals that now I can't help myself. It does look nice. Last is the artistic arrangement of pillows in shams topped by decorative pillows. When you make a bed with that much care, you can stand back and see a classy finished product. More than anything, a well-made bed tells a guest that a host has invested heart into the welcome.

I ask again: Does it really matter if we make our beds every day? Why make the bed when you're just going to mess it up again in fourteen hours? Why make it if no one is even going to see it except you? The deeper question, which I'm trying to get at in writing this little book, is this: Does keeping house even matter?

If the baby is just going to eat off that highchair

tray two hours from now, why take time to clean it now?

If I spend hours getting to the bottom of the laundry hamper, only to have someone throw in a pair of dirty socks moments later, why take time to do laundry?

If kids are going to drop Cheerios on this kitchen floor again, why even sweep it?

The futility of our work as housekeepers can lead us to conclude that we should skip the work altogether, especially if no one will know and especially if we know the work will be undone almost immediately. We can't answer the question of making the bed until we answer the question of meaning and tuck it deep into our minds and hearts, in the place where we reach to make our decisions.

My son has taken up the sport of bouldering, and he has a t-shirt that shows a hand with bent fingers that represent the grip needed for the small handholds found on boulders. The smaller the handholds, the harder the climb. We need a scripture that juts out in our minds and gives us a good handhold for why we should even do any of the monotonous, seemingly futile housekeeping chores. What truth from God's word are we going to hold onto, when we look at the bed and ask, "Why? Why make it?" A good place to turn is to Jesus' own statement, tucked into a lesson on prayer.

Jesus talks about how much the hypocrites like to pray out in public where everyone can see them and be impressed. "But when you pray, go into your room, close the door and pray to your Father, who is unseen. Then your Father, who sees what is done in secret, will reward you" (Matt 6:6). Can you hear the word for the weary homemaker? If you are a believer in God, you have in him a Father, which is a very close, tender relationship. And your Father sees what is done in secret. If you're the only one at home and you choose to make the bed, he sees your work. If you wash off the highchair tray for the sixth time, when no adult is at home to care whether you've done it or not, your Father sees your loving care for your baby. He sees, and that means it matters. It's a warm, intimate family dynamic, when you do something to please your Father. Is there any greater work than this?

We can add the question, "How shall I make the bed?" Can I just throw the covers up over the pillows? Or do I need to do hospital corners and tuck in the ends of the pillowcase all fancy? There is no legalism here. You don't have to learn hospital corners just because I did. The bed will sleep just fine without the sheet and blankets tucked in with military precision.

But if we go into the bedroom, close the door, and pray to our Father who is unseen, asking him how we should make the bed, the task is immediately elevated to something important. It becomes work done for the eyes of a King, and the bedroom is the throne room. How well shall I make the bed when my Father is watching? Can you see how all of keeping house is an act of worship? The Father cares enough to look at all the little tasks I do that no one else sees. Because he cares enough to look, I care enough to make the bed and make it well.

You are seen. What you do matters.

. 7 .
BRING THE LIGHT

You should know that I'm writing this in my office, flanked by two lights on each end of the couch, a lamp on the desk, and a "Grandma's Kitchen" scented candle burning in the window. I used the bright overhead lights yesterday when I was dusting and needed to see better, but today I'm choosing warm ambiance. Maybe you can understand, then, why I'm so cranky when I think of the condo at the ski resort. There was a huge bedroom downstairs and one lamp for the whole room—not even an overhead light.

We live in the northernmost corner of western Montana, only an hour south of the Canadian border, and for a large chunk of the year our days are very short, with about eight hours being our shortest day in December. Light in the home matters.

I learned last year about *hygge*, which is quintessential Danish culture. It means winter coziness and comfort. Did you know they burn more candles in Denmark than anywhere else in the world? They embrace the short days and long winter months, using it as a time for rest and to enjoy relationships. As soon as I heard this, I thought of my poor husband who is a sun lover and grows weary under the short, cloudy days of winter. What if I could bring Danish *hygge* into our home by adding lighting?

So, lighting it was. I tucked battery-operated flameless candles into the corners of our home, and Matt loved it! I started talking about embracing the winter coziness. Meanwhile, flickering candlelight turned the winter darkness into something to look forward to, with the timed lights turning on at five o'clock in the evening when the sun went down. The candlelight in the bedroom was soothing at the end of the day, too. It did something for our tired minds and bodies. It was a little romantic, too—just sayin'.

Do you know who the master of lighting is, though? My mother. She has more lamps and flickering candles than you can imagine, and they're all on timers. As soon as the sun starts to drop, her house lights up. She has cozy lighting, but also some lamps that provide bright, natural lighting if you want to read or work on needlework. She is the queen of *hygge*.

Let's talk about nightlights, too. One of my favorite rental cabins to clean has a nightlight in the bathroom, but not the condo on the ski resort. Isn't it a thoughtful homemaker who thinks of the one stumbling to the bathroom in the night? I have nightlights everywhere in my home, lighting the way through hallways to the bathroom.

As I say all this, I think of a decade ago when I visited Kampala, Africa, which struck me with its lack of lighting. As we drove down the city streets for the first time, I noticed small oil lamps on the tables of the street vendors. The church we visited in Uganda comes to mind, with its single light bulb dangling from the ceiling. I am painfully aware that electricity and lighting are for rich people. Buying batteries for flameless candles costs a pretty penny, I can tell you. But Uganda is on the equator, with twelve hours of sunlight every day, all year long. As a keeper of my house, living in the far northern part of the globe, I have decided that it is well worth the money to turn the long months of winter from a depressing darkness into a haven of well-lit coziness. We have the ability to craft the lighting in our homes to meet the needs of our own families.

. 8 .

DELIGHT THEM

Earlier this year, Matt and I needed a place to land for a week, so we drove across the valley to our friend's studio apartment. Several years earlier, we had toured the new property these friends had purchased, with a full view of the Rocky Mountains and peeking into Glacier National Park. On the property at that time there was only a small barn and a 100-year-old farmhouse that needed a lot of work. Amy's eyes were bright as she shared her dream of creating a place where people could come and rest and be refreshed. Over time, they turned the old farmhouse into something that deserved a full magazine layout, adding a massive wrap-around porch and window boxes filled to overflowing with seasonal flowers. Then they built a classic big red barn, with a studio apartment above to use as a vacation rental.

We drove down the dirt road, enjoying the view of snow-capped mountains in the background, and pulled in at the big red barn. Just as we were pulling up, we saw a little girl with braids slipping inside through the back door.

Unloading the luggage, we hauled it up the stairs and entered the private code for the door lock. As soon as we stepped into the rental, we saw a chalkboard with a note that said, "Welcome, Fitzwaters," with warm wishes and hopes that we would enjoy our stay.

Our eyes took in the beauty of this large, single room that was farmhouse-warm and boasting shiplap. I walked over to the island in the kitchen and saw a cake stand. Under the glass cloche was a still-hot homemade mini huckleberry pie. That explained the mission of the little miss with braids.

Still hot, you guys. We dumped our luggage, grabbed two forks, and dug into the pie. The crust was flaky perfection, of course, because Amy works magic in her kitchen. It was delightful.

I give credit to one rental owner who gifted a jar of huckleberry jam to her guests, but this barn rental was a different level of delight, to know someone was watching out a farmhouse window, waiting for our arrival, and ready to send a cute messenger over with a piping hot baked good at just the right moment. That was over the top.

Two days later, we heard a knock on the door. Braids was there, and she handed us a bakery box full of fresh, homemade frosted pop-tarts. I mean, really.

There was something else in this rental that I found delightful: two of the thickest white bathrobes you could imagine, hanging in the closet. I've been in a lot of vacation rentals, and I've never seen anyone offer guests something like this. It was completely unnecessary, and now that I've been on the cleaning side of things, I thought to myself, *It would mean a whole extra tub of laundry, if the guests were to use those robes.* But this rental owner wasn't thinking about her turn-around time for cleaning; she was only thinking about creating a spa-like environment for the weary travelers who would spend time in her barn apartment. Imagine two people dressed in the coziest of robes, eating hot berry pie while they looked out the windows at the beautiful farmland below and the mountains in the distance. This was a sanctuary of delight.

I remember that one day when my daughter was stressed over school, I went in and cleaned her bedroom for her while she was at school. Normally it was her job to keep up with her bedroom. She came in and was delighted to walk into a clean space. Cleaning her small bedroom wasn't that much work for me, but it was an unexpected gift of service that meant a lot to her at the time. Keeping house can be so much more than scrubbing at toilets and vacuuming up dust bunnies. It can be become an art, when we think a little further than just dealing with germs and gunk and ask, "How can I delight my family in our home?"

. 9 .

PREACH THE GOSPEL

A text came in one day, while I was cleaning my favorite little cabin tucked up against the Rocky Mountains, with instructions from my boss that the cabin owner wanted me to be sure and clean the dishwasher drain every two or three times I was there.

"Dishwasher drain?" I responded. "I've never cleaned a dishwasher drain in my life. Is that something responsible adults do?"

"I know," she texted back. "After she told me that, I went home and cleaned mine." Next came a picture of her disgusting dishwasher drain.

"Gross," I said. "I'm afraid to even look at mine."

Well, a few days ago I bravely pulled my dishwasher drain out of the dishwasher and was disgusted by the layers of slime built up on the outside and inside. I guess those things really do need to be cleaned. Except when I went to clean it, I found a sticky sludge that did not come off with dish soap. I asked the Google how to clean this thing and ended up filling the sink with bleach, salt, and baking soda. Then I took an old toothbrush to the drain, and the gunk came off, leaving a mucky mess in the bottom of my sink.

Allow me to compare that dishwasher sludge to the sin we hold in our hearts. It's equally built up in hidden places, and won't come away from the heart without a serious cleaning agent.

There is a song for housecleaners in the Psalms. David calls out to God for mercy, singing, "Wash away all my iniquity and cleanse me from my sin. For I know my transgressions, and my sin is always before me . . . wash me, and I will be whiter than snow" (Ps 51:2-3, 7b).

We are dirty.

But dirty things can be washed.

Dirty things can be cleansed.

Every time we clean something in our homes, we are saying amen to the gospel of Christ. Amen, yes, I am in agreement. Dishwasher drains, with a little elbow grease and the right combination of cleaning agents, can look like new again—gunk free—as can the human heart. All the obvious surfaces can become shiny again, and all the hidden crevices can be washed, cleansed.

I'm sitting in my office right now, watching the leaves fall from the maple tree like golden rain. After I get some writing done, I'm heading outside to do some yard work, because my husband looked at the forecast for late next week, and it has snowflakes in it. We're one week away from snow. This is a thrilling time of year, because the first blanket of fresh snow will cover over all my summer fails, like the embarrassing weed patch I have let crop up behind the shed. Come, snow, come—so perfectly white that I need sunglasses in the middle of winter because the reflection of the sun will blind me.

Dear God, clean me like that.

Can you see how good housekeeping is really a sermon you preach to yourself and to your family? When you dust the trim above the door, does that really matter? Yes, the dirt in all the unseen places matters. When you work to get your cleaning rag around the toilet seat hinges, removing filth from every tiny corner, you are saying, "In this house we believe dirty things can be made white as snow!" Dirty toilets. Dirty hearts.

In the cleaning storage places at every vacation rental is a supply of new kitchen sponges. I have been instructed to throw away the used one and leave a fresh one every time. Can you hear the Lord's words from Ezekiel 36:26? "I will give you a new heart and put a new spirit in you; I will remove from you your heart of stone and give you a heart of flesh." Even replacing the dirty kitchen sponge can become an act of worship, as we think about how God replaces yucky with brand-spankin' new and perfectly clean. Glory!

I've raised kids, so I know sometimes we can ask ourselves, "Why am I doing this, when it's all going to be dirty again in about thirty seconds?" The mundane, repetitive work can start to feel meaningless. Rub some gospel hope into it. We're showing our families the truth that Christ is the greatest cleaner of all, and he doesn't give up on getting us purified.

. 10 .
EXPECT YOUR FAMILY TO HELP

If you stay in a hotel, you pack up your belongings when you're ready to leave and just walk away—not so in vacation rentals. When you leave a rental, you're expected to strip the beds and make a pile of used sheets and dirty towels. You're expected to load and run the dishwasher and take out the trash. It might not seem like much, but when a housekeeper walks into a vacation rental at ten o'clock a.m. and knows that the next guests are arriving in five hours, that kind of help makes a big difference.

The woman I work for has three teenagers, and all three of them have helped their mom clean vacation rentals. I was there one day when her son and his friend helped load up all the trash from the outdoor bins of two rental cabins. Isn't this wonderful? I've heard home-ec teachers describe students who come in not even knowing how to load a dishwasher. Yet here are three teens who are able to go in and clean an entire rental, meeting their mother's high standard in a professional setting.

This makes me want a do-over as a parent. I made my kids help out some around the house. They emptied the dishwasher and had to take their laundry down to the basement. But I think for some reason I was afraid to make them work hard, as if they were fragile or something. Or probably I was too cowardly if they responded to chores with unhappiness. Now I think, *Wow, my boss's three teenagers know how to go into a rental, with a turn-around deadline, and clean the entire thing, from bedroom to bathroom to kitchen. And they haven't died.*

I would like to add that I had two of her teens in my high school Spanish classes, and they were the hardest working, most uncomplaining students I've ever had. Now that I've seen the housekeeping chores they've learned to do, I get it. That kind of work ethic in keeping house, even if it's a vacation rental, obviously bleeds into their work ethic at school. They know how to meet deadlines, and they know how to get their hands dirty and do all kinds of work, even the unpleasant.

Expect Your Family to Help

Is it fair to ask renters to do some chores before they leave a cabin or a condo? Yes. It's good to make the person who has enjoyed the property take some pride in helping get it ready for the next person who will enjoy it. In Philippians 2:3b-4, Paul tells the followers of Christ to "value others above yourselves, not looking to your own interests, but each of you to the interests of the others." What better place to start than in housekeeping?

A family member should look not only to his own interests in the house. He should also consider wiping off the toilet so that his brother doesn't have to come in to urine stains. (Keeping it real here.) Kids should consider how hard their mom has worked to cook dinner and gladly get up to help clear the table, scrape dirty dishes, and help load the dishwasher.

And a mom should consider the interests of her children above her own. By considering their interests, I don't mean what spoiled American kids find interesting, which is doing their own thing. I mean considering their greatest needs, and a great need for children is to learn to work, and to work hard and uncomplainingly. If we cave to our children's whining when they're asked to help out around the house, we're looking out for *our own* best interest, which is avoiding conflict and keeping kids happy. "Happy" isn't always in their best interest.

My friend, Lisa Jacobson, has eight children, and she has not done the dishes in her home for years. She cooks, and her children get up and clean the kitchen. And when I visit her home, I see kids who know how to work hard, not just in housekeeping but in all their endeavors. They take care of animals and yard work. They're hardworking students. And those who have left the home are successful in their careers.

A list of expectations seems fair in a vacation rental and fair in a private home. Chores are good work, as I'm still learning in my fifties, and they are a healthy part of a well-oiled home. My grown kids do well caring for their own homes now, but I wish I had pushed them harder to participate in caring for the house when they were younger. If I could send a message back to my younger self, I'd say: "Expect your family to help!"

. 11 .
BE HONEST

Over the past few years, I have stayed in three different vacation rentals in which the owners of the rental kind of lied to us, by omitting extremely important details. I am reminded of the Latin phrase about free enterprise that I learned in sixth grade: "Caveat emptor" (Let the buyer beware), but I say that's a nice way to let the seller off the hook for dishonesty.

One of those rental houses was warm, cozy, well-stocked, and well-cleaned. We were there for a Christmas getaway with our whole family, and we enjoyed setting up a Christmas tree and doing puzzles at the dining room table. But the owners failed to mention one important detail: this rental house was just one wheat field away from the local airport runway. I kept joking that our vacation stay was like in the movie

"Free Willie," when that giant whale jumped over the boy, and the boy reached up and touched its belly and felt the water drip off its body as it went over his head. I'm pretty sure we could have run outside at regular intervals and touched the underbellies of passenger jets, as they descended over our heads and landed what seemed like yards away from where we were staying.

Seems like something you would put on your rental website, for guests to consider before booking a stay: "In flight path of international airport."

Caveat emptor.

Then there was the East Texas house that boasted four bedrooms. It was lovely. One whole wall in the living room was glass and looked out on a small lake. It was a clean, comfortable place, with classy decor. The kitchen was well stocked.

Let's talk about those bedrooms, though. Two were downstairs, and they were really nice. The third bedroom was upstairs in a loft—not a big deal, except that the fourth "bedroom" was actually two queen-size beds thrown onto the floor of an attic. And the passageway to that attic was through the loft bedroom.

So, we're in Texas for our son's wedding. Despite being the groom, he is still the youngest, so the attic room goes to him and one of his groomsmen. Don't mind us, guys. Just walk through our bedroom into your attic space. Oh, and whatever you do, don't sit up in bed in the night, because we don't want any men in the wedding party to get concussions. Oh, and don't worry if the rental apartment catches on fire and you die because you're in a pitch-black attic room with no windows. We'll say really, really nice things about you at your funerals.

Caveat emptor.

Last but not least was the Oregon condominium, where we stayed with some friends when we all went to the West Coast for a wedding. Because temperatures had been averaging about 110 degrees, I called the friend who made the reservation and said, "Can you check and see if that condo has air conditioning? Because if it doesn't, I want to book a hotel with guaranteed A.C." She texted back and told me that yes, it was air-conditioned.

When we arrived in Oregon, the temperature had dropped into very comfortable temperatures. It's a good thing, because the two-story condominium had one A.C. unit in the living room. That was it. If temperatures had still been blistering when we arrived, we would have been miserable, because all the bedrooms were upstairs. That little air conditioning unit wouldn't have made even a dent in the living room at those temperatures, let alone made any difference in the bedrooms upstairs.

Caveat emptor.

Let's be honest about our homes. They are not perfect. There's an episode of *The Andy Griffith Show* in which Barney tries to get Andy to sell his house. When prospective buyers come to look at it, Andy fails to mention all the problems the house has, until Opie calls him out on it. He forces him to be honest and just come out and say what's broken and needs to be repaired. In the end, Andy decides it's best to stay in the house you love, even with all its flaws.

To the followers of Christ in Rome, Paul says, "We know that the whole creation has been groaning" (Rom 8:22). Doesn't that include the very houses in which we live? (In Montana, our house literally groans in the winter. When it gets below zero outside and that frigid air meets with the warmth of our house, the house pops and crack in a disturbing way.) Our houses suffer from the fall of mankind, which means everything breaks and wears out. Housekeeping matters, in all the details, but our houses will not reach perfection on this disintegrating earth.

A few days ago, I went to the laundry room to start a tub of clothes. (I never used to say "tub" until I moved in with my southern mother-in-law.) My eye caught a little bit of water coming out from underneath the dryer. There shouldn't be water under the dryer. We pulled out the washer and dryer and discovered a leaking connector, which had dripped down the wall and soaked a chunk of sheetrock behind the washer.

Sigh.

Do you know what we did? Put a fan on the sheetrock, replaced the connector, and pushed the washer back. So now we live in this beautiful home in a high-end neighborhood, but you and I both know that behind the washing machine is a piece of sheetrock that probably should be replaced. And there's a coffee stain in the office carpet that really needs to be professionally cleaned. And the trim on the shed needs to be painted, like . . . last year. And did I mention we're only hundreds of yards away from a massive gravel pit? The noise pollution in the summer can be bad. The list goes on. It's a beautiful house—a warm, clean home—but it's not perfect and never will be, especially as time takes its toll. So, as we strive to keep our houses to the best of our ability, let's acknowledge the flaws and feel the groaning of a world that is decaying. We can allow all the flaws and broken parts of our homes to create a longing in us for the perfection of heaven.

. 12 .
ANTICIPATE NEEDS

This summer, we rented that three-bedroom condominium in the Portland, Oregon area. It slept six, but the living room only had a couch that seated two people. That was it. I was astounded. Did the owners ever ask themselves, "Hmmm, I wonder where those other four people are going to sit when they're hanging out in the living room in the evening?"

If I had to put my finger on it, I would say the greatest quality of any host is the ability to anticipate the needs of guests. What might a guest reach out his hand for? And will he be able to put his fingers on it?

In the Texas rental where we stayed, I went to search for an iron, because I needed to press my dress for church, but there was no iron or ironing board. It was annoying to lack what I needed. I also found myself frustrated in the kitchen. Searching through the cupboards for some basic supplies and coming up empty left me wondering if the owners had ever spent a few nights in their own rental. Would they have stocked the kitchen more thoughtfully if their own search for supplies had come up short?

Three truths about God's anticipation of our needs come to mind. Paul tells us in Philippians 4:19 that God will meet all our needs. Psalm 23:1 tells us that the LORD is our shepherd, so we don't lack anything. And in Matthew 6:8, the Good Shepherd himself tells us that the Father knows what we need before we even ask for it. Can't we emulate these same qualities as we keep house? Instead of wearily reacting to the onslaught of our family's needs, we can get out ahead of them and try to anticipate and meet those needs before the need has even been voiced.

I see this anticipation of needs in vacation rentals. Some owners put clocks in the bedrooms, blow dryers and gifts of toiletries in the bathroom drawers, and everything needed to make coffee in the kitchen. The best Montana owners create a place for muddy snow boots and a place for coats to hang by the front door. One cabin I cleaned had one entire little table filled with every kind of information about the Flathead Valley that guests could possibly need: entertainment, restaurants, the best places to hike, and even an informational page about black bears. The forethought of these owners was a gift to whoever stayed there.

As a housekeeper of rentals, I was instructed to make sure there were extra garbage sacks at the bottom of each garbage can. Isn't this a small yet significant act of service? If the guests needed to empty the garbage can, we anticipated they would need to replace the sack, and made it as easy for them as possible to do that. One cabin had cute framed notes that sat on the bedroom dressers. They said, "For your comfort, extra blankets and pillows are in the drawers." The guest could have gone searching for blankets, but the owner erased the need to search. He anticipated that a guest staying in a cabin pressed up against the Rocky Mountains most likely would want more blankets, so he provided them and pointed them out. That was one of my favorite things in the airport runway rental we stayed in—they had a crazy amount of cozy blankets in the living room, and we used them all during our December stay. I appreciated their thoughtfulness.

When I stay in a vacation rental, one of my favorite things to be able to say is, "Wow, they've thought of everything." I want my own family to feel that way about living in our home: "Wow, Mom thinks of everything." I want them to reach for what they need and find it.

In Proverbs 31, we see the picture of a woman who anticipates the needs of her family. As a Montana girl, I especially appreciate the fact that when the first snow flies, the family of the Proverbs woman is geared up for winter. For me, that always meant checking closets in September, making sure the kids had boots and coats that fit.

As homemakers, we can build the habit of thinking a little further ahead on behalf of our families. If your husband uses the last roll of toilet paper, is there another roll he can easily put his hands on to replace it? If your kids come to the end of a tube of toothpaste, did you see that coming? Is there a replacement tube stocked in your hall closet? When your family needs to pack a lunch, can they find all the supplies in the fridge and pantry? Proverbs 31:27 and 29 tell us that keeping an eye on the affairs of our household is noble work. That includes keeping an eye to what's coming down the road. This noble woman can laugh at the days to come (verse 25), because she has given forethought to what's coming and has prepared ahead of time for what her household will need.

It takes a different mindset, though. We have to move from begrudgingly meeting all the immediate needs of our family to finding joy in meeting the needs of today *and* giving loving thought to what's down the road. Maybe a better word is *delight*. We can develop a spirit of delight in being able to say "Yes." Yes, you have winter boots that fit. Yes, there's more toothpaste in the hall closet. Yes, I did refill your prescription. Yes, I had your suit dry-cleaned. Yes, I bought more applesauce cups for your lunches. It's delightful to be able to say, "Yes, I thought of that ahead of time, because I love you!" Anticipation is a relief for the whole family.

. 13 .

INCLUDE THE BEAUTIFUL

My daughter-in-law had the same reaction to our Texas rental house that I did. "I'm re-decorating this place in my mind," she said, after coming in and taking one look around. The decor was all very nice, but none of it went together. Should there be a picture from France set next to a rustic Texas lone star set next to fancy stained glass? It felt like garage sale finds had been vomited into the living room, with no rhyme or reason.

House decor should rhyme.

At least the Texas rental owners made an attempt to create a beautiful space, even if I felt like they missed the mark. The ski resort condo was another story. In that entire two-bedroom, two-bath condo there was only one picture on the walls and it was set in Africa.

Every time I went to clean that place, I got stuck looking at that picture and thought, *Really guys? You own a condo looking out on beautiful Montana ski slopes and all you could come up with for the walls was a picture of a giraffe?*

When I cleaned that place, I decorated it in my mind. I would have hung a fun collection of snow hats and scarves from hooks at the front entry, for a bright spot of color and for guests to borrow when they stayed there. I would have bought a few Montana ski posters and framed them for the living room. And maybe some old skis could have been found, to decorate the bedroom walls. It wouldn't have been that hard to think "ski resort" and make the walls rhyme with that theme. Instead, this owner left his guests a cold, sterile environment.

The decorators of those two places could have taken a lesson from the owners of the two cabins nestled against the Rocky Mountains. Everything in the place said "cozy cabin," from the buffalo-plaid pillows on the couch, the old-fashioned lantern shower curtain hooks, and the black bear theme throughout the kitchen, to the rustic framing of a Glacier National Park map by the front door. Reason and rhyme.

One night, when our family was all gathered in the living room of the airplane runway vacation rental, we

Include the Beautiful

had an entire conversation around the bizarre 1960s hanging lamp in the corner—a lamp that didn't even work. I think we settled on the question, "Why?" Why did someone create this hideous thing, and why would someone in this day and age keep this hideous thing? Or if it's a treasure, why not at least make sure it functions? I dreamed of taking it to the dumpster. If only it were my house . . .

Does house decor matter? To answer that, let's step back and ask if beauty matters.

The other day, I did something out of the ordinary and set the table thoughtfully for Sunday lunch. Sunday is the day our children come over and we enjoy having all the family together. So, I spread out a tablecloth and put orange candles and some pumpkins down the center of the table, since fall was in the air. I placed the good dishes and cloth napkins around the table. As we sat down, we talked about the decorations.

"Should I light the candles?" I asked. Everyone was quick to say yes. (Lighting matters!) We all could feel the beauty of the table setting, and it added warmth and a feeling of value to our time together.

Jesus made a blunt statement, in John 16:33: "In this world you will have trouble." This world is filled with cruelty, lies, selfishness, injustice, and disappointments. It's cold out there. That's why I think beauty and design matter within our homes. We can offer a place for our families to come in out of the ugly and rest their weary eyes and hearts with the artistry of color and carefully arranged decor.

Maybe you're saying, "But I'm just not good at that sort of thing. I don't have an eye for it." That doesn't mean beauty doesn't matter, just because artistry isn't your forte. I have a friend who says she's not very good at choosing and arranging things within her home, so she asked a friend who is creative to come over and help her. They had fun working on this together. If you don't have a friend who will help, then go to the internet for home design ideas or buy a magazine. And this isn't about money either. Garage sales and thrift stores can offer what you need, without breaking the bank. Or maybe what needs to happen in your home is not getting more decorations but getting rid of some. Is the clutter and lack of intentional placement of items in your home creating a raucous painting instead of a peaceful Monet? It doesn't take a lot of stuff to create a welcoming, beautiful space for our families.

I remember reading once about a woman who was a refugee. She had lost everything and was living in barren conditions, but she found a little vase and put some flowers in it. I'll never forget that. I believe God made us with a longing for beauty, especially considering the beauty of his Creation that we see all around us. Some of that beauty needs to come inside the walls of our houses, even if it's as simple as a little vase with a few flowers in it. Our homes are a canvas that can be a refuge from the harshness of the world.

. 14 .
CREATE GOOD SMELLS

When I was finishing up cleaning the cabin that belonged to the white-glove inspector, her husband came to the door, sniffed, and said, "It smells clean in here." He smiled in satisfaction. The combination of shower and glass cleaner, toilet bowl spray, and floor mopping solution wafted through the cabin and gave evidence of my hard work over the last three hours. It was the smell of cleanliness.

The rental by the lake that we stayed at in eastern Texas boasted a fake scent. On the first night, while I was lying in bed, I smelled an overpowering fragrance that started to give me a headache. After putting up with it for a while, I finally got up and found out there was a plug-in air freshener right by the bed. I pulled it out of the wall, but the remaining scent still gave me a headache. The next morning, I mentioned something to the family, and they all admitted to having similar problems. After that, I went around the condo and pulled out a ridiculous amount of air fresheners from all the outlets. A comment about that went on my review of the rental.

That makes me think of my friend from college, who laughingly told me that the trick to having company over is to pour Pine-Sol in the toilet just before they get there, so they think you've cleaned.

My Aunt Karyn was magic. Whenever anything came from her, it always carried the faint smell of a favorite holiday. Cinnamon and cloves, maybe? We asked her how she got her stuff to smell like that, and she always pled ignorance. Did she use sachets in her drawers? No. She would never mention anything specific that made her home and possessions smell a certain way, but we all know there was something special. Not too much fragrance, mind you. Not overpowering. Just the smell of cozy. (Constantly burning candles was the secret.) She's in heaven now, and we all miss the way her hand-me-downs smelled when we pulled them out of a box. Her home and the way it smelled were all part of who she was.

How should a home smell? Right now, I have whites in the washer, so the smell of bleach is coming from the laundry room. I love it—smells like a woman has been working hard in here, smells like white socks and t-shirts.

You know what the best smells in a house are, though? Mirepoix in the skillet, hot bread coming out of the oven, or chocolate chip cookies cooling on the rack. Add a pot of coffee brewing and you're golden. This is the smell of love. I say forget pouring Pine-Sol in the toilet at the last minute, if you have guests coming. Instead, get some garlic and onion sautéing on the stove right quick. The aroma says, "I'm preparing something yummy for you." Smells tell their own story about work and care, and authentic aromas are better than contrived aromas.

Smells in a home need to serve the preferences of the people who live there. Some people love scented laundry soap, but those heavy fragrances tend to bother my husband and me. For the most part, I try to stay away from things with a fragrance. But I do like the way the house smells when I've spent the day cleaning. I use Windex to clean just about every surface, and it's a rewarding smell at the end of working hard. We live with my mother-in-law and her sister now, and they don't like candles with a heavy fragrance, so I don't burn those. Although right now I have a candle burning here in my office. The fragrance is called "Grandma's Kitchen," and it's the one scented candle I really enjoy. But I'm careful only to burn it here in my personal space for a short time and not out where it would bother them.

Of course, we love the smells coming from the kitchen. I like to cook, and the smell of dinner on the stove is the gift I offer to my husband when he comes in from a hard day of work. My grandma's house always smelled just a little like bacon fat, and it was the best. When I stayed the night at her house, the smells of a huge breakfast would waft down the stairs and wake me up in the morning. Bacon in the skillet and hot waffles on the griddle were always waiting for me, along with fresh-churned butter, a glass of whole milk fresh from the farm, and a side glass of grape juice or orange juice. Grandma would pull out her huge Bible and read a few verses while I ate a farmer's portion of breakfast off vintage plates. There were equal amounts of calories and grandma-love in that kitchen, and the smell of bacon went with me as a memento of those rich times with her.

Here I'll mention that my husband and I have asked the ladies with whom we live to pickle beets when we are not home. The smells in our house should be a pleasant service to our families and not a plaguing annoyance. We definitely draw the line at pickled beets.

On the sixth day of Creation, God created the human nose. I wonder what the Garden of Eden smelled like? For five days God spoke things into being, where there hadn't been things before, and when he was done, he looked at what he had made and uttered that Hebrew word, "*tov.*" How could *tov* not include all the smells of lush, green, growing things? The smell of blooming things. The smell of rich soil. When Adam and Eve turned their hearts against God in sin, I wonder if their exit from the garden came with a great sorrow over the missing aromas that accompanied "*tov.*"

When I was growing up, there was a miniature potted orange tree in our house. At a certain time of the year it would blossom, and the fragrance went straight to my soul. And I'll never forget when my mom would let me pick one of those oranges—the way the juice would squirt as I broke into the peel and the immediate wafting of fresh orange scent that would reach my nose. A house in this world is no Garden of Eden, but my mother's orange tree was a nod to it. Can we, in the grace of Christ, restore good smells to our families, within the walls of our own homes? Can we offer up to noses the hope of all that is clean and good?

. 15 .
GIVE YOURSELF A GIFT

I was sitting in a vacation rental that I had cleaned meticulously from stem to stern. Everything was done except the last load of laundry and then mopping my way out the front door. It smelled squeaky clean in the cabin (try finding that in a candle scent), and I was enjoying the fruit of my own labor, at least for ten more minutes before the towels were ready to be folded and put away.

Because everything was done, I was free.

I was free to sit down and do creative work, clicking away on my computer with ideas for this little book. This is what happens when we clean at tornado speed and finish our housework: we can do something else. We can put up our tired feet, look around a clean house, and be free in mind and body to tackle something new or something restful.

Booker T. Washington, a man of incredible accomplishments, said, "As far as I can, I make it a rule to plan for each day's work—not merely to go through with the same routine of daily duties, but to get rid of the routine work as early in the day as possible, and then to enter upon some new or advance work."[5] There is something to the idea: if we get our daily duties done, it frees us to do something new or something more advanced than the routines of housekeeping. It frees us to sit with a picture book and a child on our lap, cuddling in a relaxed frame of mind because we know our housework is done. It frees us to call a friend and say, "How are you doing?" It frees us to read a chapter in a book or play a song on the piano or sit on the front porch and watch the leaves fall. Can we get rid of the routine work as early in the day as possible?

In Proverbs, a command is barked at us: "Go to the ant, you sluggard; consider its ways and be wise! It has no commander, no overseer or ruler, yet it stores its provisions in summer and gathers its food at harvest" (Prov 6:6-8). In other words, get up and get your work done at the proper time, and then you can enjoy yourself at the proper time. You have no idea how many times I've recognized my own sluggardly tendencies. (I can't believe that *sluggardly* is an actual word.) When I can tell I'm being a procrastinator on household chores, I say out loud to myself, "Go to the ant! Go to the ant, you sluggard!" How embarrassing if a bug knows how to get his routine duties done and out of the way better than a grown woman does. These proverbs are here for us, like sermons that fit in one's pocket, to help us live well in the moment. They memorize easily, and we can preach them to ourselves at a moment's notice. And we need constant reminding, to do the unpleasant housekeeping first and then to enjoy rest or to pursue some new work.

Today I chose the dinner menu for the week, made a grocery list, went and did all the shopping at two different stores, came home, unloaded the car, put everything away, and washed the grapes and the lettuce. Meal planning and shopping are always my big Saturday chores, and the process takes about three hours, from start to finish. Now that I'm done, I have a few hours this afternoon with the freedom of mind to sit down and craft this chapter. That includes having another little cup of coffee and resting before church tonight.

When my house is a mess and chores are undone, I am a mess and I am undone. If my office trash is climbing up the wall because it's been so long since I emptied it, my insides feel like they're climbing up the wall. A mountain of unfinished housework affects my mind and bogs me down emotionally. Shame creeps around my heart and cripples me from truly resting or truly accomplishing any good new endeavor. The only prescription for clearing the mind and heart is to get up and get with it. Clean that toilet. Fold that pile of laundry. Make that bed. Just get it done. Then comes freedom.

. 16 .
MAKE REPAIRS

On my very first day of being trained to clean vocational rentals, my boss and I arrived just as the renters were loading their vehicle to leave. I passed the dad, who was wearing a firefighter t-shirt.

"I want you to know there are no working smoke alarms in this condo," he said.

My boss apologized and said she would look into it. But then I found out that the owner of this condo tends to ignore the plea for repairs. What if there had been a fire in the condominium complex while the guests were there?

That was the same condo I revisited by myself a week later and couldn't get in the front door—not a very welcoming entry to a vacation rental. My boss finally had to call the building superintendent, who came and strong-armed the front door until it opened.

"Here's the problem," he said. "Someone broke this door jamb, so now it sticks. The owner needs to repair this." The same owner who wouldn't take care of the smoke alarms? The same owner who wouldn't replace the old, nappy comforters on the beds? The same owner who was allowing the paint to peel on the bathroom baseboards? Let's not hold our breath waiting for a door to be repaired.

One of my great joys in being a housekeeper has been learning how to fix stuff. Just the other day, I asked the Google, "Why is my toilet handle so hard to push?" and ended up watching a very helpful YouTube tutorial video. Soon I was on my way to Lowe's, searching for toilet repair supplies and looking at different toilet flush seals. Who knew there were different sizes of those and that you needed to know what kind of toilet you had? I went back home, looked at the toilet brand and took off the old seal, went back to Lowe's, and found a perfect match. In no time, I had the toilet seal replaced and everything put back together. Did you hear the angels singing when I was able to flush so easily? It felt great to take care of something that was broken.

We need to keep up with the simple repairs that are

needed in our homes. Proverbs 14:1 comes to mind: "The wise woman builds her house, but with her own hands the foolish one tears hers down." Can we talk about our hands? They're either holding a new toilet flush seal, or we're sitting on them. Sitting on your hands is all you have to do if you want your house to start crumbling around you. You don't even have to do any work to destroy your house; just let the constant needed repairs slide. A woman who builds her house belongs, literally, in Lowe's or Home Depot.

A few weeks ago, when I discovered that the washer had been leaking, Matt and I pulled it away from the wall. He diagnosed the problem as a leaking connector hose. It was the weekend, and he had to work all weekend. I pulled out my keychain-sized Stanley tape measure (women who build their homes need one of these in their purse) and measured the hose, then made yet another trip to Lowe's, where I found the water connector aisle and bought a universal connector. At home, I read the instructions and replaced the hose. The instructions said, "Check to make sure it doesn't leak." I checked, and it wasn't leaking, so I pushed the washer back in and voilà: repair made.

I can't write this chapter without talking about my all-time favorite substance, called Sugru. Please order yourself some. If a wise woman builds her house, she needs some of this magical stuff. It's moldable glue that turns into a waterproof silicone rubber. I am a crazy woman about this and always keep some on hand. I have used it to fix the long rip in the lawn mower bag, the break in the bottom of the dishwasher silverware rack, and the broken dryer vent handle. I even used it to build a new handle for my mother-in-law's slow cooker, a new leg for the rotisserie oven, and a new shelf support for the fridge shelf. Sugru awakened something creative in me, and now I'm saying regularly, "I bet I can fix that!"

My dad always used to fix everything, but now I'm realizing that the ability to build and repair is in me, too. I've taken that mindset into the vacation rentals with me. One day I was making the bed in a cabin, when I found a rip in the seam of a pillowcase. I was going back to turn over that cabin again in a few days, so on my next trip I took thread and a needle. In just a few minutes, I sewed up the rip in that seam. Another time, I noticed that one of the shower curtain hooks was missing. As I was cleaning, I found the broken pieces in a cupboard. I tucked those pieces into my cleaning bucket, took them home, glued them back together, and returned the repaired hook to that cabin the next time I went. It was so rewarding to see the shower curtain hanging evenly again. I fixed those things be-

Make Repairs

cause I've developed a habit of seeing what needs to be repaired and taking care of it as soon as possible.

You know how quickly our homes disintegrate before our eyes. It's because we live in a world that is broken. But we can develop diligent minds, keeping our eyes open for things that need to be repaired, and learning our way around educational tutorials and hardware stores. What one thing is in disrepair in your own house today? Do you believe you can fix it? Get up and figure it out. Get it done. To the best of our ability, we can build our houses as we live in them.

. 17 .

BE EFFICIENT

"Clunky" is the only way I can describe my first days of cleaning rentals. One of the cabins had all its supplies in a separate garage, and I must have made thirty unnecessary trips back and forth to the garage. I thought to myself, *You've got to get better at this. You're wasting too much time.* So, I got out my phone when I returned home and made a list of all the supplies I would need from the garage in order to clean that rental. The next time I went, I pulled up that list, gathered everything at once, and saved myself a whole lot of steps. Efficiency matters when your boss is paying you by the hour.

I feel embarrassed, realizing that when I clean my own house, I work a little, read a little, work a little, watch a little Hallmark, work a little, check my email, work a little, stare out the window at the birds. After cleaning a few rentals, I thought, *Huh, I can do a whole lot of cleaning if I don't allow anything to drain my efficiency.* It took being on the clock for me to learn this.

The other day, I decided to clean my own bathroom as if I were getting paid by the hour (in my dreams!). Would you believe that I finished it in record time? Because I cleaned like it was a rental instead of in my normal walking-a-dog-who-needs-to-stop-and-sniff-everything style. (Maybe not the best imagery when I'm talking about cleaning a bathroom, but you know what I mean.) What I'm saying is that I just cleaned the bathroom, from start to finish. I didn't stop to organize a drawer, which is the kind of minutiae that often sidetracks me. I also didn't stop to sit down and take a break. Can you imagine if I were to work this efficiently on a regular basis? Wow.

When I clean a rental, I've learned a lot of efficiency tricks, too. Most importantly, as soon as I walk in, I immediately get the bed linens into the washer and make sure the dishwasher has been run. If those two things don't happen, it can mean a lot of lost time down the road.

My boss taught me to go in and spray down the shower and the toilet first, to get those things soaking in cleaner while I do a few other chores. I would add that it's more efficient to clean those two places, if I first grab a square of toilet paper and clean off all the hair. (Nothing makes me gag like dragging hair around with a rag. Gross.)

It's such a small thing, but it also helps to get a cleaning supply bucket with a handle. When I started my rental cleaning job, I needed to be able to grab everything and put it in my car, for easy transport. It's nice to have all the supplies in one bucket at home, too. As for supplies, using minimal cleaning supplies means minimal thinking about what to use every time you clean something. I like to use Windex to clean just about everything in the bathroom and kitchen, because ammonia works great. My boss gifted me with a Norwex cleaning cloth, teaching me to get a corner of that cloth wet and wipe down the glass, then use the dry part of the cloth to wipe off the mirror—streak-free in less than a minute. So in great irony, I use that for the mirrors and don't need Windex.

And may I get on a soap box about the glory of towel hooks versus towel rods? I spend an inordinate amount of time in vacation rentals, folding towels just so over a rod, and layering them with a hand towel and a washcloth. But in my own house, I replaced the towel rod with a row of hooks, because the family can toss their towels on those with no need for special arrangement. It's a simple way to increase efficiency.

Oh, and how about plastic containers in the kitchen? A few years ago, I got rid of all the odd-sized, random plastic containers and spent thirty dollars to replace them with a few different sizes of matching containers. Now I adamantly refuse to let any random container in our plastic storage drawer. This allows efficiency in emptying the dishwasher, efficiency in matching containers to lids when it's time to put food away, and efficiency in being able to stack leftovers in the fridge.

There's also an efficiency of what I call house "real estate." There is prime real estate in kitchens and bathrooms: the countertops and the easiest-to-access cupboards and shelves. Efficiency means you put the most-used items in the top real estate locations. Maybe it's at this point that I should confess that I *know* I'm an efficiency freak. My brain is constantly asking, *How could this be arranged for easier access? How could this be organized better? How could my habit or system of cleaning and working be streamlined?* Maybe normal people don't think this way, but hey, it's why I'm writing a book! Let me be the crazy, and a little bit of my efficiency brain can rub off on you.

If we reach for a Bible verse for encouragement regarding efficiency, I would go to Paul's words in Ephesians 5:15-16: "Be very careful, then, how you live—not as unwise but as wise, making the most of every opportunity, because the days are evil." That phrase "making the most of" means to redeem or to buy for oneself. Would you like to buy yourself the opportunity to be able to go on a bike ride with your first grader? Be efficient in your housekeeping. Would you like to buy yourself time to take a friend for coffee? Be efficient in your housekeeping. Would you like to buy yourself the opportunity to give your husband your full attention? Be efficient in your housekeeping. A little extra time spent creating efficient systems now can save you a lot of time later—time that can be spent doing new and valuable activities.

. 18 .
SIMPLIFY

My friend works at a home decor store, and she told me she's in charge of managing the "dust collector" section. When she said that sarcastically, something inside me was immediately offended, because I have, ahem, a few dust collectors in my home. Right now, it's autumn, so I have cute little pumpkins strategically placed around my home. Now why couldn't she have called these "adorable decorations" instead of giving them a cleaning rating?

Here is a simple fact: when I cleaned vacation rentals, the homes with the least amount of clutter and "adorable decorations" were the fastest and easiest to clean.

One cabin I cleaned was tastefully decorated. The owner is an artist, so there were fantastic prints of his pictures everywhere, and his wife had set around themed decor that was a beautiful complement. This was all lovely, until I had to dust the place. In contrast, the condo at the ski resort boasted only one picture and nothing adorable anywhere, but it's amazing how quickly I could move over the surfaces with a duster when I wasn't needing to move things.

The Shaker style appeals to me greatly, and I do lean toward minimalism in my own home. But I also have some favorite decorations that I like to pull out. My mom has a lot more "adorable decorations" than I do, but my daughter and daughter-in-law have way less. Certainly, beauty is in the eye of the beholder. But what I'm driving at is that the more cuteness we set out, the harder it is to clean.

This leads to the question, "How much time am I willing to spend cleaning?" Going back to Paul's command to the followers of Christ, are we able to redeem opportunities that are eternally meaningful or are we wasting opportunities because we're spending so much time managing all the stuff we've accumulated in our homes? Only you can answer this question for yourself.

In an earlier chapter, I made the point that there is a place for beauty. We can create a beautiful environment where our families can rest, and I think some of our decor becomes somewhat of a comfort to our families. I know I feel this way when I go to my mother's house. She changes the decor for every season, and it feels very much *home* when I walk into her house in July and see all the patriotic decor, and red, white, and blue M&M's in a cute jar in the kitchen. But at what point does beauty tip over into a burden of housework?

It's certainly worth it to me, in the bleak midwinter, to dust around a ridiculous amount of flameless candles. The infusion of light into the home makes it worth the clutter. But sometimes I wonder, when I'm trying to wash grease off the decorations we keep above the top cabinets in the kitchen, if it's worth the beauty in that space. It's a lot of work to get on a ladder, bring everything down, wash it, wash the cabinet tops, and then get it all back up there. Our stuff creates work for us.

Keeping house includes managing the belongings our children have, and simplifying means we get to decide how much stuff our kids have and what they're allowed to get out at one time. A few weekends ago, my daughter and I spent half an hour going through the toy closet at our house. I live with my mother-in-law and her sister, so that toy closet has been what the youngest three grandchildren have enjoyed over the last years. They have now moved away and are getting too old for most of those toys anyway, so it was time to decide what my 18-month-old grandson should play with. I took a huge bucket of toys to the crawl space, which left two plastic bins of age-appropriate toys and a few buckets of blocks. When my little guy comes over for a day at Grandma's house, I pull out one of those plastic bins and one of the big trucks for him to play with. It's enough, and when he leaves it makes cleanup much simpler. *Enough* is a good word, don't you think?

Have you ever looked at what the Shakers did in their homes? No useless decorations. Only what was simple and useful was placed in a room. Of course, their simple and useful pieces were beautifully made. I've had a picture that was my grandma's, and it's a framed picture of a room in a Shaker house. Irony. Shall we stop and think about the raised eyebrows a Shaker woman might have given, on looking at that picture? She might have thought, "Well, now you're going to have to dust that." I love the framed image, though, because it speaks to me of what can be, if I am willing to have less. In pictures of Shaker-style houses, I always notice the windows, but if the rooms were full of decorations, would I even notice those beautiful windows? Is there a tipping point, where we start to lose beauty the more beauty we try to add to our homes?

As we take valuable time to ponder what housework should be in our own homes, let's ask two questions. First, do I have a good amount of beautiful items in my home or could I use a little more or a little less? If the clutter of decor is becoming wearisome to the eyes instead of restful, I could work to bring down the sheer number of decorations. Second, is the amount of stuff in my home a reasonable amount to clean or is it so much that it's stealing opportunities for me to do more meaningful activities? If cleaning has become a burden, simply because of how much stuff I have, then it might be time to box up some items and make trips to the thrift store. Would less be better?

We get to design our homes, and this includes the amount of work we design for ourselves. Can we learn from the cabin with a little too much decor and put up fewer pretty things, while not going so stark as to hang only one ill-chosen picture in the house? God gives us minds for choosing and hands for arranging. Let's ask Him to help us find the balance between beauty and simplicity.

. 19 .
WASTE NOT

In every vacation rental I went into, there was a Swiffer with a disposable cleaning pad. Each of those cleaning pads would barely clean the floor in one room before it dried out, which meant I had to change the pad as I went from room to room. Cha-ching. Cha-ching. It was so convenient, but cost so much money over time, and my zero-waste heart cringed every time I threw away another cleaning pad.

There are a lot of disposable cleaning products on the market right now, and they are wonderful. They're so easy to use, toss out, and just replace with a brand-new something: disposable dust mops, disposable toilet bowl scrubbers, disposable sponges for the sink, and disposable mop pads. The purpose of all these is to make life easier, and they do; they make cleaning fast and easy.

But is this the best use of money over time? It's not just cleaning items that end up in the garbage. We also have paper towels, paper napkins, and plastic garbage sacks. How much money are we spending on items that are used once and then tossed in the trash?

There's another reason why I cringe, though, besides the hit to the bank account. It also pains me to think of all those replaceable cleaning products ending up at the dump.

Maybe you're a city girl, but I'm a Montana woman. My husband has a Ford F150, and we often drive the ten minutes to take stuff to the landfill. We've lived in the Rocky Mountains for almost three decades, and we've watched the garbage mountain grow to a disturbing height over the years. It's sobering to back up with a truck bed full of garbage and watch a row of other trucks do the same. I always think about how much garbage is landing on that pile in one day, multiplied by 365 days a year. With the coming of COVID-19 into the world, we watched the population in our valley grow by 30,000 people in one year, and I wondered what that would mean for the landfill. Imagine that many more women throwing away all their disposable household items.

In Genesis, we see the creation of the world. "The LORD God took the man and put him in the Garden of Eden to work it and take care of it" (Gen 2:15). Man is supposed to take care of the earth. I think that's why I feel sad when I go to the dump, and why my soul cringes to add to what's there. It seems small, to think of one woman being more careful what she throws away. For me, it's not that I can change the world by washing and reusing plastic freezer bags; it's that God has embedded a sense of responsibility in my soul, to take care of this world. My thoughtfulness regarding waste in my household is an act of personal worship. It's a deep understanding that I am a steward of Creation.

When I started cleaning vacation rentals, I was given a disposable dust mop to use, but I couldn't stand the waste. I went shopping and found a microfiber dusting mop that slides over a rod, so I bought two of those for only about five dollars each. The handle lets me stand flat-footed to dust (no wasting time getting a stepladder to reach light fixtures), and I can dust through several rooms so fast (hurray for efficiency!). The dust mop comes off and goes in the washer. Because I bought two, I can dust again without worrying whether the first duster has come through the laundry yet. For ten dollars, I now have a tool I can reuse for years. I also bought a bunch of inexpensive garage rags in the Wal-Mart auto section, to use as cloth napkins instead of using paper napkins. When the family comes over for Sunday lunch, we use cloth instead of disposable paper napkins. A small investment for reusable items can mean years of less waste.

When I was home to visit my mom last, I joined her in running errands. We drove out of town to the dump with a car full of recyclable materials, and I helped her put all that she had sorted into its appropriate bin. She had put a lot of effort into this, creating space in her garage for recycling and taking the time to learn about what is recyclable, including cardboard, paper, plastics, and glass. I know you might live in a place that requires recycling, but Mom and I live in states that do not have any such requirement. For us it comes down to the heart of the matter. Should we be conscientious housekeepers who consider the waste in our homes and choose to do something about it?

Sometimes my efforts to reduce waste feel futile. Does it really matter that I filled a kitchen drawer with rags and use those instead of paper towels? Does it really matter that I wash and reuse freezer bags until they die? Is there significance in choosing to use wool dryer balls instead of disposable dryer sheets? Does it make any difference that I stopped using disposable paper plates and cups? Should I go to so much effort to make sure the garbage sack is completely full before I take it to the dumpster? Sometimes I feel silly that I care so much about this.

In the end, I trust that the Lord of Creation sees my heart. He knows I care and that I'm trying. I have not achieved zero waste, for sure, but I'm slowly making changes in that direction. My heart acknowledges the Creator and embraces the task of tending to my tiny plot of land.

. 20 .

MANAGE THE FRIDGE

"It's one of the perks of the job," she said, as she opened the vacation rental refrigerator. "If the renters have left anything in here that you think is good and you'd like to take home with you, it's all yours."

"Wow," I texted her, the first time I cleaned a rental by myself. "I didn't know what you meant when you said perks." Then I sent her a picture of a fridge shelf full of beer left by the renters. This condo was on the third floor, and the garbage was on the sub-floor. It took this Southern Baptist preacher's wife three trips to get all that beer down to the dumpster.

My own refrigerator has become, over the years, sort of a protected space, like a national park or bird wetlands or an elk refuge. It's a place that never used to get much of my attention but now is a focal point and an important location deserving of care.

Lewis is my best example of why I watch over and protect my fridge. Lewis Parker is nineteen months old at the time I'm writing this. He can say "Grandma," and his dimpled hands can reach up to the doors of the fridge but can't yet open them. I open my fridge door and reach for cheese or blueberries or cherry tomatoes or leftover "no-no's" (noodles) for this precious little guy. Feeding him is a great privilege of being a grandmother.

The fridge is where my grown children go, hoping for free and easy food. (I don't think they'll deny this.) A mom's fridge is where adult children find a wealth of leftovers and a rest for their bank accounts.

The fridge is where my husband looks for an evening snack or a quick lunch.

The fridge is where my mother-in-law and her sister keep their pickled beets and favorite salad dressings and cracked wheat bread.

The big white storage cooler in the kitchen isn't just a place to keep food cold. It's a place where we can feel Psalm 23:1-2a: "The LORD is my shepherd, I lack nothing. He makes me lie down in green pastures." The human equivalent of a green pasture, in my mind, is a clean, organized, well-stocked refrigerator, where the

Manage the Fridge

people I love can go to feel, deep in their hearts, that they lack no good thing. Caring for this space is how I love my family.

So, every weekend I clean out the refrigerator. I pull everything out, wipe down the shelves, and wipe out the bins. I throw away anything that's bad. I face all the jars and bottles outward—a habit I learned when I worked at a grocery store back in my college days. (Have you ever noticed that everything on grocery store shelves is neatly turned to face labels forward? Can you imagine how long it would take you to shop, if no one took the time to arrange things in an orderly way?)

There is a defined place for everything in our refrigerator. The leftovers are always on the same shelf. The bread is always on the same shelf. The cheeses are in one bin. The fruits are in another bin. The veggies are in another bin.

When I buy groceries, I cut carrots and put them in a plastic container filled with water, for easy snacking during the week. (Thank you to my daughter-in-law for the water tip on keeping carrots fresh.) I wash the lettuce and put it in a plastic container, for easy salad making during the week.

When I open the refrigerator during the week, I always take five seconds to make sure it's orderly. Admittedly, this is in part because I am obsessively an organizer, but it's also because this space has become an important hub of feeding my family. I want them to feel the goodness of cleanliness and organization every single time they open the fridge doors, easily putting their hands on what they need. I want them to feel the goodness of the Shepherd who is providing green pastures for them.

Caring for the fridge has led to less waste in our home. Being able to see what's available, in a clean, appealing way, means that food gets eaten instead of lost in a wasteland of dark and dirty corners. Looking after the refrigerator is connected to our stewardship of resources, and it is meaningful work we can do as housekeepers.

I will encourage you that caring for the fridge weekly and then five seconds here and there throughout your day is not that hard. It is not a massively time-consuming work. This is simply a habit that takes time to develop; it certainly took me several years to get to the routine I have now. But if you will make your fridge a protected refuge for food, your family will be impacted in a positive way.

. 21 .
PRACTICE HOSPITALITY

Hospitality was a word that always triggered defeat in my heart. It was in the category of "things I stink at." My introverted self loves my guests so, so much, but I quickly get so, so weary of hosting and just want to be a hermit.

Hermits are not hospitable.

But a family stayed with me many years ago, and when they left, the mom wrote me a note about how amazing I was at hospitality. What? I mean, WHAT? She seemed sincere and not just trying to be nice to me, but I had a hard time believing her words were for real. Cue the personal mantra: "I stink at hospitality."

Not too long ago, I was talking with a fellow pastor's wife, and we got to reminiscing about how many people we had hosted in our homes. It surprised me to name the college-aged summer missionaries we had hosted over the years. Wow, that was a lot of people. And as I thought about it, I said out loud, "They all really enjoyed staying with us. But I wasn't much of a host. I just treated them like family."

She said to me, "Maybe that's why they loved your house, because you treated them the same way you did your family."

Hmmm.

Then I got this job cleaning vacation rentals—the job I knew I was going to hate, except I didn't hate it. Do you know what my favorite part of that job was? The last two minutes, after I mopped my way out of the house and stood at the front door ready to leave. When my boss was training me, she said, "This is when I stop and say a prayer for the next guests." We bowed our heads, and she prayed for people whom she would never meet. I loved that so much.

I loved the way it felt, in every tiny cleaning action I did, to think of how the coming guests would feel about it. I imagined a woman seeing the neatly folded toilet paper square on the toilet roll. I imagined the clean, taut sheets giving a sense of welcome for a tired body at the end of the day. I imagined the guest reaching for a clean towel, neatly hanging by the shower. All this made me so happy. Was this hospitality?

Where did my mantra of failure come from? I think from comparison. There are people in my life who just kill it when it comes to hosting people in their homes, and I am not like them. For example, my mother-in-law is the queen of hospitality, and she dotes on people from her kitchen like nobody's business, tending to their every need. But me? I tend to say, "Hey, if you want soda to drink, go get it out of the garage fridge." All those summer missionaries we hosted? I would show them where the food was and say, "Help yourself." And I expected them to help themselves. Oh my goodness, my mother-in-law would never do that! We are so different.

Here is where I'm going to tell you something very important, and you will want to write it down: hospitality can look different on different people. (I'll wait while you find a pen.)

The way I keep house and welcome guests will always be Christy style, and that is okay.

Recently, I hosted a retreat for the women of my church. I'm the women's ministry director, so I planned this for months. The day of the retreat, I went out to our church camp hours early to set up, bringing with me an overflowing truckload of decor and snacks and activity supplies. For four hours I worked by myself, laboring to turn the utilitarian camp lodge into a welcoming home. I brought almost my whole home with me, from decorations to bar stools, to pretty serving dishes. On the plastic tables, I laid out Pinterest-worthy centerpieces complete with flameless candles that we turned on every evening. Fresh flowers went on the mantelpieces. I put feminine touches in each of the main bathrooms. I even brought my seven-foot framed chalkboard to put behind the podium. This was thrilling work for me, and I was deeply happy. With all of my heart, I wanted my sisters from church to walk in and feel the beauty of the place. When I was done, I gave a satisfied look around and thought to myself, "I do care about hospitality, and I've done a good job here." It was a moment when I recognized that God had been working in me, to change my inner mantra of failure to a mantra of successful obedience.

Peter tells the followers of Christ: "Offer hospitality to one another" (1 Pet 4:9a). Keeping house means opening the door to others and being generous to them, and it's an attitude that is portable. I found I could be hospitable to others by cleaning their vacation rental in a careful, detailed way. I could practice hospitality in the way I planned a retreat for women. (Did I mention I baked sixteen dozen cookies?) Hospitality is an ingrained attentiveness to whatever guest is under our care at the moment, whether within the walls of our home or outside of it.

Do you know where I think the best hospitality comes from? Knowing the hunger for home yourself. I remember when my husband and I were in college in Texas, and my home was in Wyoming. An elderly couple from church invited us over, and we ate dinner on TV trays in the living room. I wanted to weep. A couch! I was so homesick for a living room and a couch and a casual dinner on TV trays. By Instagram standards, the hospitality rating on that evening was one star, but for me the normalcy and simplicity went down to the deepest place in my lonely heart, and I left that couple's house feeling like I had tasted home.

Let's keep house generously, whatever that might look like for us. We can keep one eye on the needs of our own families and one eye on the needs of others who might pass under our care.

. 22 .

CLEAN SMARTER

Mopping has been an exasperating job for me. Because my mom always mopped our floors on hands and knees, with a bucket of suds and a rag, I've always mopped the same way. My mother-in-law and her sister were horrified the first time they saw me do this—worried that I was going to destroy my knees. I assured them I am in no danger. But just between you and me, my fifty-something-year-old knees are starting to feel the difficulty of mopping by hand, and I have always procrastinated on mopping because it is so physically difficult. I also refused to use a disposable mop pad, even though they sure were fast and easy to use when I cleaned vacation rentals. But they're just so wasteful. And I've refused to use a floppy mop, because how in the world can that thing get into corners well? (Matt rolled his eyes when I told him this, but hey, caring about the corners is what makes me great at cleaning!)

But recently I found something I think just might be the ticket. It was on my daughter-in-law's birthday list, so I did some research. It's a steam cleaner that requires no cleaning fluid except for water. It has a rectangular head like those disposable mops that are so awesome, but it comes with washable microfiber covers. It gets into the corners, but without the waste.

"Hey little elf," I said to my daughter, as I was wrapping the steam cleaner for my daughter-in-law's birthday, "could you tell Santa I reaaaaaallly want one of these for Christmas?" I have high hopes of receiving the gift and of its efficacy in cleaning floors well.

I'm also remembering my misery over cleaning baked-on food from the walls of the microwave. It was one of those jobs I dreaded and avoided, because it required so much scrubbing. But one day I read the advice to heat a mug of water in the microwave for four or five minutes and let it sit for a few more minutes. It steams off all the dried-on food, which is then easily wiped away. Again, steam was a free cleaning product; I just needed to know how it could be applied in my cleaning routine.

God made a woman's brain, and I believe we

should always be reaching for more knowledge about the craft of homemaking. Are we doing our work in a smart way? And is it possible that gaining knowledge about keeping house can be an act of love for the Lord? Consider how Jesus defined the greatest command in all of scripture: "Love the LORD your God with all . . . your mind" (Matt 22:37). What does it mean to show love for the LORD with our minds when it comes to caring for our homes? It means thinking and learning.

One time I visited my sister-in-law in Texas. She has never had a dishwasher, which makes my jaw drop every time I think about it. We finished a meal, and I saw her fill the sink full of suds. Then she scraped dishes and put them in that soapy water to soak. Aha. I was watching a woman who had never enjoyed the appliance many of us own, but she had learned how to take care of dishes in the smartest way possible, soaking them so she wouldn't have to scrub dried-on food when she got to the dishes. She developed a habit that was the wisest choice in her situation. She used her brain.

I told you about that mammoth bunk bed in the ski resort condo, didn't I? The full-sized bunk bed that was so high I could barely reach the top mattress while standing on my tiptoes. Eventually I ran out of energy and just stood there, with my arms resting on the wooden frame, bawling in frustration like a two-year-old. Once Matt talked me out of my despair, he said, "Next time you clean this place, why don't you take a stepladder?" He is brilliant. I took a stepladder like he suggested, and it was ten times easier to make that bed when I got up there where I could reach it. All I needed was a new idea for tackling that task in a smarter way.

Of course, thinking requires some perspective. We usually have to step away from chores for a time and just think about them, before smarter, more creative housekeeping methods become apparent. Learning takes time and a reaching of the brain for information. Visiting my mother and enjoying her stack of magazines is often a time when I can read and think, pulling in new information about how best to do things. Cleaning vacation rentals also took me out of my own home environment and forced me to think about my housekeeping routine in a completely new way. Housekeeping is largely manual labor, but to be done well it demands intelligent women who put thought into the best way to do those manual tasks.

How do we work smarter in our homes? It begins by asking: How do I work smarter? Am I using the best tool? Have I developed the best method? Am I doing this task the hard way? Is there a better routine? A better product? A better mindset? A better day and time?

This can be our demonstration of love for the Lord: using our brains to improve our craft of keeping house.

Magazine stands are filled with housekeeping tips. They shout "how to clean it faster," "how to organize it better," and "how to make housework easier." These headlines can express a woman's desperation: How can I be less trapped by housekeeping? The search for how-to tips sometimes comes out of a desire to escape the mundane. But what if we lean into learning as an act of love? *Lord, show me how to keep house smarter.* What a beautiful whispered prayer this could be, to offer God our minds regarding keeping house.

. 23 .
SEND A MESSAGE

In the cozy rental cabin nestled against the Rocky Mountains, I was washing the cute little outhouse-shaped salt and pepper shakers, when I realized one of them had wording that implied a cuss word. Immediately, my impression of the vacation rental went from a feeling of warm hominess to a feeling of coldness and crassness. One word had an effect on me. It was jarring and disappointing.

Our homes send a message. One of those messages comes through cleanliness, organization, and decor; it's a communication that is subtle and implied. The other message is in actual words that our families and our guests read. We live in a time when it's common to hang signs in our houses. In the bathroom, we see plaques that say, "Wash your hands." In the laundry room, we see plaques that say, "Wash, dry, fold, repeat until you die." We literally post our attitudes around the house. What message are we putting in front of our families?

I have a giant chalkboard in my bedroom. It's seven feet long and framed in barn-red wood. As a wordsmith, it makes me happy to write Bible verses and encouraging quotes on that chalkboard. Those words are the last thing my husband and I see before we go to sleep at night, and many times the words written on the chalkboard have been a short sermon we've preached to one another before turning out the lights.

For a very long time, my mom had a little note stuck on her dryer at home. Obviously, it was something that inspired her, but I don't think she knows how much it has become a part of my own thinking. It said, "Eat less. Do more." Over the years, I've watched exercise programs and fad diets come and go, but my simple health plan has remained "Eat less. Do more." That little saying often has been the motivation for me to go take a walk. It has been the reason why I've refused a second helping or why I've chosen the smaller dessert. I'm sure my mom hung those little words for her own reminder, but she passed them on to me without ever speaking them aloud. I never knew where she got that quote or what made her hang it, but I feel the effects of it decades later in my own life.

In one of my daughter-in-law's first years in our family, she gifted me a tiny frame, with wording in it that she painted herself. It says, "We are deeply loved." Normally I rotate out my decorations, but I can't seem to put this one away. Every time I look at it, I can feel the reminder that God loves me very much, and I always seem to need to hear that. *Oh right, I forgot how much I'm loved*, I always think to myself. Even the smallest of words can have a surprising amount of impact on the heart.

Recently, we stopped in at Selah Farms, to visit our friend who owns the vacation rental above the big red barn. We were visiting with her in the living room, and I saw a small chalkboard that had adventures listed on it, with some of them crossed out. When I asked about it, she said those were all the fun things the family hoped to do that summer, and as they completed them, they crossed them off. They live on a farm with a massive garden, hayfields, cattle, pigs, and goats. Their work is sunup to sundown, but they had carved out hopes of fun for the family. These words echoed the proverb that all work and no play makes Jack a dull boy. What if that had been a list of chores? The choice of words shaped the family's summer.

Paul tells the believers in Ephesus a "don't" and a "do." He says, "Do not let any unwholesome talk come out of your mouths but only what is helpful for building others up according to their needs, that it may benefit those who listen" (Eph 4:29). Certainly, these commands carry over into housekeeping. Do we hang words on the walls of our homes or scratch them onto chalkboards or paint them, frame them, and prop them on the bedroom dresser? If any part of our home displays words, there should not be unwholesome cuss words. Signage should build and benefit. It should teach and encourage. As we stock the pantry with food and the bathroom cupboard with toilet paper and toothpaste, in consideration of the basic needs of our families, so we should stock our homes with words that benefit mind and heart.

All that said, I'm not a big sign person, but I do have a few favorites. One is a picture my friend gave me that's called "God's Fingerprint." In small gold lettering, the artist has created a large fingerprint made of one verse about God from every book of the Bible. I hung it in my bathroom, and every time I brushed my teeth, I read one of those verses. The art created an opportunity for me to worship God.

A second sign is one I found when I was shopping with my mom in Wyoming. She listened to me ooh and aah over it and indulged me by buying it for me. It is a simple statement in black typewriter font on a white background, framed in black: "Worry is the misuse of imagination." It never fails that when I see that sign, I just happen to be worrying, and it reminds me to stop and imagine how God might want to solve whatever problem I'm anxious about. It's an echo of Jesus' command that his followers are not to worry about anything.

But my all-time favorite sign is one that could be engraved on my headstone, because it is everything I want my life to be. It carries three commands etched into a rectangular piece of weathered, barn-red wood: "Pray hard. Work hard. Trust God." For fifteen years, that sign hung in the entryway of our house, above the coat closet, and I hoped my family and guests would hear my voice as they read the words. I longed for the commands to be a perfect match for the lifestyle I was modeling within the walls of our home. Now we live with my mother-in-law and her sister. My "home" is now a bedroom and an office, but I've hung that sign above my office door. Even though keeping house has changed for me in this new setting, I want the words and the sentiment to come with me.

I'm a writer, so I know about editing. Editing means rereading with careful eyes and a red pen, to make sure everything you're saying is meaningful and articulate. We need to edit the words in our houses. Is anything crass or negative in tone? Delete. Or maybe you've never thought about how valuable words can be. Could you bring scripture or encouraging sayings into your home in some way? Don't overlook the valuable overlay of influential words in your home.

. 24 .
STAY IN MOTION

When we were newlyweds, we went to visit other young married friends in their college apartment. It was a very grownup thing to do. While we were visiting, the wife got up and started dusting the living room. I remember how this impressed me. We had her full attention as we chatted, but she busied her hands with a task that needed to be done. It was one of those things I tucked away for what I wanted to be like when I grew up—making good use of time.

When I took physics, it was one of the few left-brained classes where there were moments when I grasped and remembered information. One of those pieces of information that stuck was Newton's first law of motion: if a body is at rest, it will remain at rest; if a body is moving, it will keep moving unless something stops it. (That's how I remember it.) Let's apply this law of physics to keeping house: if a woman's body is sitting on the couch, her body will remain on the couch; if a woman gets up and gets moving, her body will keep moving. You just can't argue with that, can you?

But there are different kinds of movements. We like to watch dance competition shows at our house, because we love the art of movement and expression. That said, we've become quite the (self-proclaimed) experts on different types of dances. We know how to pronounce *pas de deux*, and we've seen crumping. We can differentiate between contemporary dance, locking and popping, disco, and Bollywood. It's fascinating what one can do with the human body. Keeping house is also a dance, and we get to decide what kind of movement it is. There are frenetic, fast-paced movements and there are slow, graceful, fluid movements. In my mind, keeping house is like a smooth ballet.

One time I was interviewed for a Canadian TV channel. (I'm sure you remember it.) The interviewer told me that people were so busy, and how did I think we could stop being so busy? I paused and told him that I didn't think God always intended us to be less busy. I had just finished reading a whole stack of amazing missionary biographies, and, from what I could see, those admirable men and women filled the hours of their days with meaningful work for the kingdom of God. I told the interviewer that I thought the problem was what kind of work we were doing and how we were going about it. It was not the answer he was hoping for, and that led to an abrupt end to the interview.

Regardless of our good efforts to grow in efficiency and to work smarter, there is still an endless amount of housework to do. The job is never done. But the answer doesn't lie in striving to decrease the workload but in developing the mindset that we have been entrusted with an extremely important but demanding job that requires us to keep moving most hours of the day. We can also see ourselves making graceful, fluid movements like a ballerina—working beautifully and with quiet strength throughout our homes all day long. You'll think I'm ridiculous, but I often picture myself like a gifted dancer, stretching out my arms to put away laundry and bending to pick up grandbaby toys off the floor. I can hear the orchestra playing beautifully in the background.

There are times, though, when I have serious bathroom-cleaning to do, and it calls for some old work clothes and fast moves. That's when the AirPods go in my ears and I turn on music with a good beat. Sometimes I dance a little while I'm cleaning, which I would never admit to publicly. Still, whether to fast or slow music, acting as a dancer feels very different from grunting our way through labor like we're slaves under a whip.

Maybe I should have titled this chapter "Use Your Imagination Well." If we imagine that housework is some kind of horrible torture, we're likely to remain inert on the couch. But if we imagine ourselves dancing through our homes all day, and we add fitting music to what we imagine, it brings an appeal to getting up and moving around.

My grandbaby was just here, and he is Mr. Destructor. I got out one little plastic bin of toys for him, but he spread them to every corner of the known universe. I found a hot pad on the windowsill—pretty sure he's the one who put it there. He loves books, so it looked like a public library exploded in the living room. And he was just here for one day. His momma has to clean up after him every day, again and again and again, all day long, until he's old enough to learn to clean up after himself. Even then, we all know that for a very long time she'll have to be a very close instructor, as he learns to clean up his own messes. What kind of dance is this constant tidying? It can be frenetic and burdensome or smooth and artistic with a lot of heart and rhythm behind it.

In the beginning of time, we see that "the Spirit

of God was hovering over the waters" (Gen 1:2). This means that his Spirit was moving, fluttering. Is it any wonder that from this God we get Newton's first law of physics? God was moving, and he has continued to move within his Creation. God made us in his image, so it seems a good imitation of God that a woman would hover over her home—fluttering over all the tasks that need to be done, in a position of constant forward movement, to build and create something wonderful.

We have to start moving and keep moving. A load of laundry should always be running. There are always dishes that belong in sudsy water. A surface is always gathering dust. The beautiful, clean, organized home demands a caretaker who is constantly walking, bending, reaching like a dancer. This movement, in keeping house, reveals the very imprint of the living, moving God.

. 25 .

BESTOW HONOR

It was my first cleaning job. I had been assigned the downstairs bathroom in the condo at the ski resort, and my manager was tackling the upstairs bathroom. As I was finishing up the cleaning, I sat down on the toilet seat and carefully folded the end of the toilet paper square into a dignified line. My boss would never know I did this, but it's something I've often done in my own home when I have a guest coming. If the fancy hotels do such a thing, why not me? When I was finished, I went upstairs to see what needed to be done next. My boss sat down on the toilet seat and said, "There's something I want to show you that I always do with the toilet paper."

"Already done," I said smugly.

Let's talk about the art of the unnecessary. I am

confident that a vacation rental guest could use the toilet paper just as well without it being folded all fancy on the end. But what happens when we take time with these little unnecessary details? We elevate the experience for the guest by showing that he or she is worth our attention.

That ski resort condo was the worst. There was no honor in it for the guest—no attention to little details by the owner. There were no decorations except for a picture of a giraffe in one of the bedrooms. In the kitchen was a bizarre collection of mismatched glasses. It was a sterile and cold rental.

In contrast was the cute cabin I cleaned the next week. There was honor in that place, in many forms. One was at the coffee station, where the owner had provided every coffee condiment and a full array of K-cups. In this coffee-drinking culture we live in, is there any better way to honor a guest than by making sure we've provided for all their coffee needs?

Another simple yet honoring touch was the guest book laid out on the dining room table. A guest book is totally unnecessary, but it invites a guest to tell his story about his experience in the temporary home-away-from-home. It quietly communicates, "We want to hear from you. Did you enjoy yourself? Were you comfortable? Do you have any criticism that would help us make a better experience for the next guest?" One cabin I cleaned had a very expensive leather guest book with leather tie straps. It was luxurious, and it shouted, "Your experience matters to us!"

I compared the sterile condo at the ski resort to these cabins with their guest books and concluded that the sterile condo shouted, "All we care about is getting your money so we can pay this mortgage and make a buck!"

The cozy cabin owned by the white-glove lady had a basket on the table, and I was instructed to make sure to fill it with some granola bars and a jar of huckleberry jam. That huckleberry jam had to be ten dollars a jar—a completely unnecessary expenditure—but this woman honored her guests by her extravagance.

What about honoring our own families by the way we manage our homes? Recently, a family member was ready to reclaim an antique dresser we had been borrowing from her. This left my husband without a dresser that had also been doubling as a nightstand. I put a lot of thought into what a perfect nightstand would be for him. At a consignment store, I found one that was just the height he wanted. When I brought it home, I arranged the nightstand so the lamp was at the level he wanted for good reading at night. I filled a jar with the throat lozenges he often likes to use. I also put his breakfast bars into a container on the nightstand, so that when I bring him coffee in bed in the morning (a service I offer joyfully), I can easily get him a breakfast bar, too. It was just a nightstand, but I tried to honor Matt in thinking about what would fit his needs.

Honor isn't just for big people. I have a toddler in my life now who calls me Grandma, and he and his momma come every Wednesday to spend the day. I have honored this little guy by clearing three shelves for his books, topped by a puzzle and a big plastic car hauler. There are squeezy snack pouches in the pantry, and he knows where to find them. Outside there is a toy backhoe waiting for him to enjoy. He is an honored guest in our home.

It takes extra thought, beyond clean toilets and fresh bed linens, to create a house that honors the people who live there. We have to spend time thinking about what would make each person feel important, and we have to be willing to take ridiculous, unnecessary steps to add honoring elements that fit each person. This is great spiritual work, though, because we are instructed by Paul to "honor one another above yourselves" (Rom 12:10). I'm sure that Paul wasn't picturing fancy toilet paper folds or welcome gifts of huckleberry jam, but as homemakers, we get to shape what honor looks like in each room of the house, being thoughtful toward each person who will live and move in that space.

. 26 .

GROW SOMETHING

The email said, "Who wants some shamrock bulbs?" I replied a quick, "Me!" Later in the afternoon, I went to the school administration office, and Jill gave me some little bulbs wrapped in a wet paper towel and tucked into a sandwich bag. With great hope, I went and bought a pot that was the size she recommended. With joy, I filled the pot with soil, buried those little bulbs, and watered them. Every day I peeked into the pot. Sure enough, in a few weeks, two little shamrocks poked their heads out of the soil and promptly died. Nothing else ever came up.

I marched that pot full of dirt out to the garage and stuck it in the back of a cupboard.

About a month later, I was hosting a women's event at church, and I had the women divide into groups based on their ability to grow things. There was a green-thumb group, a plant-killer group, and a group for women who wanted to learn. It just so happened that a friend brought me a paperwhite bulb that night as a gift. (At first, I thought she said "paperweight," but I have since been educated about the narcissus flower.) After the event, as I was holding the paperwhite in its beautiful glass vase with rocks on the bottom, I bemoaned my deceased shamrock, and one of the green-thumb girls told me that her grandpa said never to give up on shamrock bulbs. She diagnosed my plant as needing more light to live, and encouraged me to go home, pull it out of the graveyard in the garage, and give it another go.

I took her advice and put the pot of dirt in the bay window above the kitchen sink, where it would get full sunlight. Soon I had green shamrock shoots poking their heads above the dirt, and every week since then, a few more shoots have been added to their number. I now feel hopeful that in time my little gray pot will overflow with shamrock happiness.

Plants require care and knowledge, and it may seem to some women that there is enough care of people required in keeping house, without adding the stress of keeping something leafy alive. But have you ever looked up the health and psychological benefits of having houseplants? Do you know that even NASA recommends having a lot of houseplants? It's fascinating to Google "plant benefits" and find tons of articles about the science of air purification, the respiratory benefits from increased humidity, and even the boost to healing, attention, and mood. Maintaining house plants is more than just a hobby or decoration; it's an investment in the wellbeing of our families.

This isn't surprising. When we open to Genesis, we see God taking one entire day to speak vegetation into existence. "The land produced vegetation: plants bearing seed according to their kinds . . . and God saw that it was good" (Gen 1:12). Plants are a significant part of our earth. I can feel echoes of God's creative work as I water the eight plants in our kitchen bay window every Saturday. I can see that vegetation is good. Certainly, watching plants flourish is therapy for my own soul.

Vacation rentals don't have plants. I've cleaned a few rentals that had silk plants, but living plants require constant love and tending. They need a steady routine of watering. They need someone to talk to them affectionately and someone who will trim off dead leaves. They need someone to notice that their toes have reached the end of their shoes and it's time for a bigger pot. Plants belong with families, not transient renters.

Growing plants has been a learning curve for me. I learned that my prayer plant is tropical, and it has grown marvelously in the bathroom next to the steamy shower. I finally figured out that the fuzzy, unidentified plant in the kitchen barely needs any water. And I had to look up how to water my air fern. (Matt insists that the air fern is fake and that I just keep getting it wet every week for no reason.) I still don't know why the mother-in-law's tongue refused to produce any new leaves. It is now deceased. But I may try that plant again down the road, except with a little more research next time. Right now, I have an aloe vera plant, but the tips keep turning black. I need to figure out what I need to change in caring for that plant. There's always something new to learn, when you're trying to grow things.

One fun plant to enjoy for a short stretch of time is basil. In the produce section of my grocery story, they sell fresh basil that is still attached to roots and dirt. You take it home, put the root ball in a glass jar, and cover the dirt with water. Then you can cut fresh basil leaves to put on your pizza or into your pot of chicken. And the smell of fresh basil is wonderful. I think even a self-proclaimed plant killer could manage to keep a basil plant alive for a few weeks.

One of our most stunning plants is a Christmas cactus that is right above the sink. My mother-in-law has had this plant for a long time, and it blooms a few times a year—usually in step with when Hallmark starts their Christmas movies. Have you ever looked closely at the blossom of a Christmas cactus? It is exquisite. When this plant is in full bloom, doing dishes turns into an act of worship for me. My hands are in the suds, but my eyes are delighted by the blossoms in front of me. I can't help but turn my heart to the Lord who spoke a plant like this into existence. He declared this to be good.

God said plants are "*tov*," which, I remind you, means "good" in every sense of the word. If we are going to care for our homes, it makes sense for us to bring this goodness inside. We can do this slowly, one plant at a time. It doesn't have to be expensive. In my neck of the woods, pots can be found at thrift stores. Dirt doesn't cost much. And the friends with green thumbs love to share shamrock bulbs and other plant starters. Some of our ladies at church had a perennial party last year, where they all brought perennials from their gardens and shared them with one another. Think of all the benefits of having a wealth of vegetation inside your house, and go plant something.

. 27 .
RAISE THE VALUATION

I was the first one up from the Thanksgiving table, putting on my rubber gloves and filling the sink with suds. My dear friend of many years, who was visiting from Texas, grabbed a dish towel and started drying.

"You're doing the dishes. You've changed," she said.

"I'm not the same person I used to be," I replied soberly.

She was there when I was writing my very first book, *Blameless*, a compilation of the ways I was seeing God taking me from a life of shame to a life of good, blameless living. So much of that book centered on keeping house, because shame seemed to live in every corner of my housekeeping story for so many years. "Slowly, slowly," as they say in Israel, God has helped me to develop skills and self-discipline and a better work ethic, so that I am no longer ashamed of my housekeeping. Now I'm the one jumping up to tackle the mountain of dirty dishes.

Dishes have been an interesting journey. I remember back in the day, when I let the dishes go so long that I discovered Texas-sized cockroaches crawling on them. I remember how many times we ate out, because my kitchen was so dirty that I couldn't even begin to make dinner. That was the old me. Scripture tells me that because I'm in Christ I am a new creation (2 Cor 5:17), and I can feel it as I rinse a gravy-covered plate and load it into the dishwasher. Who is this new woman?

As I type this chapter, my temporary stint as a vacation rental cleaner has come to an end, and I have since found employment as a part-time assistant at a compounding pharmacy. My work includes doing quality checks on medications, entering logs into the computer, answering the phone, and handling checkout at the front counter. But do you know what it also includes? Dishes. We're a compounding pharmacy, so our technicians are making medications from scratch. It's fascinating to see them fill pills with powder, concoct creams, and even make lip balms. But all that creating requires the use of spatulas, beakers, pill-measuring equipment, and glass mortars and pestles. A few times a day, I find myself donning rubber gloves and grabbing a brush to scrub laboratory dishes. I'm getting paid to wash dishes.

It's tempting, I'll admit, to bemoan the fact that I have a college degree and used to be a professional teacher. I find myself, once again, asking if doing dishes really matters. Does keeping house in a pharmacy really matter?

But a technician came over to me the other day and said, "Thank you for doing this. It's so helpful." (Thank the Lord for people who speak value over our work.) As I scrubbed a spatula that was covered with some kind of medicinal cream, I thought about how my simple (menial?) job was allowing the technicians to stay at their work of filling the mountain of prescriptions that were waiting in the queue. That's the great value in doing housekeeping. What we do forms a base that allows others to live and work and be who they are. A base is at the bottom of things, acting as a support.

At our house, we enjoy watching *Shark Tank*. We've also learned a thing or two about making business pitches, because the dreams of entrepreneurs are often shot down on the show when they present ridiculously high valuations of what their businesses are worth. Housekeepers do exactly the opposite on a regular basis—they develop a valuation of their role that is ridiculously low. How much is "menial" worth, anyway? Toby Mac wrote a song entitled "Speak Life," a song that I would sing over the homemaker who feels her endless dishwashing and laundry work and sweeping are meaningless. Toby says we can turn our hearts with the very words we say. Which way does your heart turn?

You know that steam cleaner I was hoping to get for Christmas? Well, it's December 26, and I didn't get it. Sad story, I know. For some reason, my husband didn't think buying me housekeeping supplies was a very fun Christmas gift. (You know I'm not going to fault him for that.) But I did get money for Christmas, so I'm buying the steamer for myself. Ha. I got onto the website, and part of their sales pitch was "Everybody hates cleaning." What kind of talk is that? What kind of valuation? The marketing copywriters were implying that cleaning was some horrible, dreaded task. I wanted to rewrite their sales pitch.

When your hands are in dishwater, what are you saying to yourself about the work you're doing? When you're wiping down the baby's high chair for the umpteenth time, what are you speaking inwardly?

When you're pulling yet another load of whites out of the dryer, what value are you placing on that task? I beg you to keep the word *valuation* handy and use it to shape the language you choose regarding the keeping of your home.

. 28 .
KNOW WHEN TO NEGLECT

The hardest part about cleaning vacation rentals was that I had to do all the work expected of me every single time. Of course my employer expected a complete cleaning sweep in exchange for a paycheck. But it's different at home.

I'm a diligent housekeeper, but I have times when I purposefully neglect large portions of housework. Some of those times are seasonal. In the late spring, I always do the quintessential spring cleaning, because when summer hits, I'm going outside. We live in northern Montana, so our summer lasts about three seconds, and I'm going to spend those three seconds digging in flower beds or sitting on a riding mower, not dusting ceiling fans and mopping the laundry room floors. I don't feel guilty about this, and no one gasps because a bit of grime develops over a couple of months.

When I was teaching school, I would do a good late-August house cleaning. Then, for a few weeks after school started in September, I would do nothing but go to school and come home to collapse in exhaustion, trying to re-acclimate my mind and body to going to work. It wasn't the time to worry about my housework, except for making sure everyone had clean underwear and some kind of food to eat. I would eventually get in the groove and become a housekeeper again, with a crescendo of cleaning energy in November, just before the holidays.

This December, I found myself in a state of exhaustion, after one of the hardest years I've ever experienced. My mind felt inflamed from thinking about so many hard things for so long. My body was weary from hit after hit of stress and sorrow. My heart was broken from the year's hardships and weary from powering through difficulties. So, I gave myself the month off from everything I possibly could. What do you think of that?

We need rest, and that is part of keeping house. As housekeepers, who will give us this time off? Only ourselves. If we are managing the ship, then we are the ones who have to know when to drop anchor and just be still. I'm 52, so I know from experience that the long journey of keeping house is benefited by taking personal vacations from the work, and no one is the worse for wear when we do this. In fact, our families benefit when we, as women, become adept at taking breathers, because seasons of refreshment help us function better in the long run. I'm not talking about laziness and just being a slacker when there's work to be done. I'm talking about understanding the seasons of life and the state of our souls and bodies. One is foolishness; the other is wisdom.

Do you mind if I refer to Andy Griffith again? How many of those old, black-and-white episodes show Andy and Aunt Bee and Barny and Opie out on the front porch, after Sunday church, doing nothing. Aunt Bee is a hardworking, fastidious housekeeper, but she sits in a rocking chair and does nothing on Sunday afternoon.

She does nothing.

Doing nothing is an art practiced by the wise. Surely, we are intelligent enough to look at our homes and know when it's time to kick it into gear and when it's time to let things slide for a bit, for the sake of mental, physical, and spiritual rest, and relational investment.

In my new job at the compounding pharmacy, I am working with younger women who have young families. They work full time and then go home to care for their homes and children. Housekeeping has to look different for them than it does for me, because I work part time and don't have little kids at home. They must neglect something, because they don't have enough hours in the day to be full-time employees and the world's best housekeepers and loving wives and caring mothers. To neglect is to choose the best way to spend one's time when time and resources are limited. Wise neglect is a skill, I say.

My mom is hosting us for Christmas this year, and I'm sitting in a cozy chair in her front room as I type this chapter. Before we arrived, she traveled out of state for a week, for a December wedding, and then came home and kindly helped two friends who were under the weather. She bemoaned the Christmas disaster that had exploded in her living room but knew that helping her friends was how God would have her spend her time, instead of finishing Christmas preparations and preparing for company. I applauded the neglect of her living room mess. Neglect is always a good choice when we wisely displace keeping house for better, more necessary work.

Neglect is a skill of assessment. We assess the housework that needs to be done, the people who need to be cared for, and the state of our own health, and we make careful decisions about where best to put our time and energy. Some things move to the top of the to-do list and some get moved to tomorrow's or next week's to-do list or maybe next month's. Purposeful neglect must always be part of a wise woman's housekeeping plan.

. 29 .
RUB IN GRATITUDE

Some stains are harder than others to remove. I made several passes working on the dutch oven we used for Christmas Eve potato soup, which scalded on the bottom because we forgot to turn off the burner. First, I let it soak. Then I used a scraper to get off the thickest layer of burned milk. Then I let it soak again. Then I scrubbed with the kitchen scrub brush, but that wasn't touching it. Finally, I broke out a Magic Eraser (some disposable products are just too good not to use) and invested some elbow grease, which resulted in a clean pan. Phew.

Keeping house carries a layer of drudgery that is not easily removed.

Don't women often gather and complain about cleaning house? Mom and I were chatting this morning about the miserable job of cleaning the shower. We live in lands of hard water, where calcification is a constant problem. We use squeegees after every shower, trying to keep soap scum and hard water from accumulating. Mom has made a habit of spending ten minutes on the shower every day. Oh my word, that sounds like some kind of torture. But trying to get a few weeks of calcification off the shower is equally miserable. Groan.

Normally the last thought—my very last thought—would be to stop and be grateful for indoor water and a shower in my house. Complaining and moaning are my first response and those attitudes need a soak, a scrub, a Magic Eraser, and some elbow grease to get rid of them. Replacing them with gratitude for having something wonderful to clean never comes naturally. Which is more difficult? Cleaning a shower in a land of hard water or scraping the griping off your heart and mind?

This morning, my friend in Africa sent me pictures of their family's Christmas feast. I was reminded of my trip to Africa a dozen years ago, and of watching a child carry a jerrycan of water from the community spigot to his house. It was beyond my comprehension then, coming from rich America where indoor plumbing and clean water is what even poor folks consider standard. My friend's Christmas feast pictures included a shot of one of his daughters stirring a large pot over an open flame out in the yard. I can promise you that when I was scrubbing at the burned Eagle Brand milk that I accidently spilled on my stove burner a few weeks ago, I was not thinking, *Thank you, God, that I have a stove in my house.* I was just grumbling over the mess and how long it took me to clean it.

When I was cleaning vacation rentals, the work was exhausting. It revealed how out of shape I was. But at some point, I thought to be thankful that I was physically able to do a very physical job. I was lifting huge baskets of laundry and carting them up and down stairs, and I was grateful that I could do that. I thought about the young man I met who had cerebral palsy and who had never known life outside a wheelchair. Thank the Lord for my arms and hands and back and legs and feet that function and allow me to move from task to task.

A few weeks ago, tornadoes wreaked havoc through Kentucky, just as we were coming into the holidays, and my heart aches for those who have suffered the loss of their homes. I imagine the women who have lost so much, and how they would give anything to have a toilet and sink to clean again. I also have thought much about the Afghan refugees who recently fled their country with only the clothes on their backs. Seeing this kind of suffering puts my own home into perspective, underlining what a great blessing it is to have a house, with sheets to change and woodwork to dust and floors that need to be mopped. I am humbly grateful to the Lord for the privilege of having a house to manage, because I know a house is something that can be gone in an instant. I'm sure my reader friend, who barely escaped the Paradise, California fire of 2019 with her life, would give a hearty amen to this little sermon on gratitude.

I just went with Mom to the grocery story, and I played the spoiled child and begged a latte off her. As the barista was steaming milk, Mom pointed out to her that there was a coffee spill on the floor near one of the tables.

"Toss me a wet rag and I'll wipe it up," I said. The barista refused to let me help, but I would have been glad to do it. Who am I? How did I go from the prima donna of my younger years, who didn't want to get her hands dirty, to this woman who would have been thankful for a chance to help with some housekeeping in a coffee shop? My legs are young and strong enough for me to get down on the floor to wipe up a coffee spill, and I'm thankful for that. I'm thankful for the opportunity to help someone else with my ability to clean. Moaning and procrastinating used to be me, when it came to keeping house, but the slow work of thankfulness is starting to displace those crusted-on layers of displeasure.

Are you a thankful housekeeper? Try rubbing some gratitude into each chore and see if a mindset of thankfulness doesn't transform your life as a homemaker.

. 30 .

KEEP IMPROVING YOUR CRAFT

At my age of 52, I just finished my stint as a vacation rental cleaner, and I cannot believe how much I learned and grew as a housekeeper by doing that job. I've been keeping house for over thirty years. Who would have thought I still had so much growing to do?

When I got married in 1991, I had no idea that keeping house was a complex job that required knowledge, skill, a Bible-based attitude, and deeply entrenched good habits. I wish someone had said to me, "Keep working at it. You'll get the hang of this." Instead, I mostly felt like a failure at everything. As I mentioned, several years ago, I wrote a book called *Blameless: Living a Life Free from Guilt and Shame*. I think of this new little book on keeping house as an addendum to my earlier message. In Ephesians 1:4, we read that God has always intended that in Christ we would be "holy and blameless in his sight." Looking back at my first book, I'm amazed at how much of my journey toward blameless living still centers around keeping house. I guess that's because keeping house is such a big part of my life as a woman, and it's connected to my heart, mind, and soul.

But I would add some new information about what it means to grow in skill as a housekeeper. That is the idea that we can always be learning from one another. In Proverbs we read, "As iron sharpens iron, so one person sharpens another" (Prov 27:17). We have good effects on one another, and I don't believe there is an end to that process. One woman can always sharpen another woman's housekeeping skills, if the latter woman is humble enough to believe that she always has something to improve and to learn.

Here's a simple example: I always used to spray one part of the toilet and then wipe it down. Spray, wipe, spray, wipe, spray, wipe. Then I was trained to clean rentals and saw my boss grab the toilet spray and spray down every part of the toilet in one fell swoop. She turned and did the same with the shower. Letting those soak in cleaner for five minutes or so, she went off and did something else. Then she came back with a couple of wet rags and wiped down the shower and toilet, lickety-split. *Aha*, I thought. Now I grab the Windex, spray down the entire toilet, and walk away to do another task. Then I come back and wipe it all off. It's a small change, but it's a big deal, when I think of how many of those little tricks of the trade I've learned from other women over the years. They add up.

We had family friends over for lunch the other day. I watched the two older women do dishes together over the kitchen sink. "You know," said the friend, "I figured out that if you use a Magic Eraser on the sink, it cleans it up really well. You should try it." Sure enough, a day later my mother-in-law grabbed a Magic Eraser and scrubbed down the kitchen sink. It removed a filmy white layer that had developed over time and brought the sink back to looking as good as new. Now, I want to point out to you that both of these women are master housekeepers, and they have been at the job for, um, let's say quite a bit longer than I have, but they still showed a mindset of willingness to learn to do something better. One had a new tool, and the other was humble enough to give it a try.

How old are you? How long have you been keeping house? You don't have to answer out loud. But do you believe that at your age and place of experience, you could become sharper at keeping house? Maybe you have all the skills and it's your attitude that could use some changing. Or maybe you have the skills but haven't turned them into steady habits. Or maybe your attitude is good but your knowledge base is small, and you just have a lot to learn. Part of our journey toward holy and blameless living is making sure we remain students.

As a former schoolteacher, I know there is joy in mastery of a subject. It was so fun to take beginning Spanish students from zero knowledge to an ability to speak complete sentences in the new language. But in between zero ability and the celebration of skillfulness is labor and tedium in learning. May I suggest that the same is true in keeping house? There is celebration ahead (as I'm now enjoying in my fifties), but it was 365 days a year for thirty years of dusting, vacuuming, organizing, decorating, scrubbing, tossing, and folding that was the road to the good housekeeping I now enjoy. They say it takes 10,000 repetitions before you become a master at something. That's 10,000 toilet scrubbings, 10,000 loads of laundry, and 10,000 dishes to put back in the cupboard. And with those repetitions comes a whole lot of trial, error, and the need to learn better methods from someone. Learning is long, hard work.

Keep Improving Your Craft

My hope, as you finish this little book, is that you feel encouraged to keep trying to improve how you keep house, no matter your age or how long you've been at this. Can you feel all the meaning from scripture that is wrapped around the work we do in our homes? It all matters—down to the smallest, most menial of tasks.

Thank you for caring for your home.

ENDNOTES

Epigraph
Louisa May Alcott, *Little Women* (New York: Simon & Schuster, 1982), 138.

Chapter 1: Get Therapy
Elisabeth Elliot, *Suffering Is Never for Nothing* (Nashville: B&H Publishing Group, 2019), 45–46.

Chapter 2: Discover the Treasure of Solitude
Maria Konnikova, *Mastermind: How to Think Like Sherlock Holmes* (New York: Penguin Books, 2013), 26, 132–133.

Chapter 5: Allow for Perfection
Booker T. Washington, *Up from Slavery* (Grindl Press, 2013), 123.

Chapter 15: Give Yourself a Gift
Booker T. Washington, *Up from Slavery* (Grindl Press, 2013), 113.

Made in the USA
Middletown, DE
04 March 2022